The Master

Exploring the Sermon on the Mount

by

Roger Aubrey

Copyright © 2017 Roger Aubrey

All rights reserved, including the right to reproduce this book, or portions thereof in any form. No part of this text may be reproduced, transmitted, downloaded, decompiled, reverse engineered, or stored, in any form or introduced into any information storage and retrieval system, in any form or by any means, whether electronic or mechanical without the express written permission of the author.

ISBN: 978-0-244-90994-9

*For Jim and Paulette Harkins
Shining examples of the Masterplan*

Also by Roger Aubrey
The Circle of Life
Discovering God
Stars and Sand
Angels
The Elijah People
The Little Book of Hope

Roger Aubrey was born and raised in Cardiff, Wales. He lives in the city with his wife Dianne. Roger has been a Christian since 1966, and is a member of All Nations Church. He also visits churches and Bible Colleges throughout the world, teaching the Word of God and building up the Body of Christ. Roger has a PhD and Master's degree in Christian Doctrine from Cardiff University. Roger enjoys various sports, photography, and spending time in the great outdoors. He likes to read biographies of those who shape history.

Author's Note
The reader will notice that I have replaced the term *the LORD* in the Old Testament scriptures quoted in the book with the name Yahweh, which is the original Hebrew word that *the LORD* translates. Yahweh is the personal name of God that he has revealed to us in the Old Testament; it is his covenant name. Yahweh sounds like the Hebrew phrase 'he is', hence God calls himself I AM WHO I AM (Exodus 3:14). In John 8:58 Jesus declared himself to be Yahweh when he said, 'Before Abraham was born, I am!' Yahweh describes God as the infinite, unchanging God; he is the same yesterday, today and forever.

Unless otherwise stated biblical quotations are taken from the Holman Christian Standard Bible.

My grateful thanks to Kier Adams for the cover design.

At the end of each chapter I have included some questions as a basis and stimulus for personal consideration or group study and discussion. Feel free to use them in whatever environment or setting possible.

Contents

Introduction: The Masterplan
1. What is the Sermon on the Mount?
2. Blessed: The Beatitudes
3. The Poor in Spirit
4. Those who Mourn
5. The Meek
6. Hungry and Thirsty for Righteousness
7. The Merciful
8. The Pure in Heart
9. The Makers of Peace
10. The Persecuted
11. For My Sake
12. The Salt Covenant
13. Light of the World
14. Turning Point
15. 'I Could Kill You'
16. I Only Have Eyes for You
17. Marriage and Divorce
18. Yes and No
19. Turn the Other Cheek
20. The Extra Mile
21. The Power of Love
22. Secret Givers
23. The Secret Place
24. Our Father in Heaven
25. Praying the Kingdom
26. Necessary Bread
27. The Power of Forgiveness
28. Testing Times
29. Kingdom - Power - Glory
30. True Fasting
31. You Can't Take it with You
32. Perspectives and Priorities

33. Specks and Logs
34. Dogs and Pigs
35. Keep on Keeping on
36. The Golden Rule
37. Gates and Roads
38. Bitter Fruit
39. Doing Father's Will His Way
40. Solid Rock

INTRODUCTION

When he saw the crowds, Jesus went up the mountain, and after he sat down, his disciples came to him. Then he began to teach them saying... (Matthew 5:1-2)

For many years I approached the Sermon on the Mount with a certain degree of apprehension and sometimes with a large amount of frustration. As I read the words of Jesus and discovered what he expects of his disciples, I'd find myself swaying between the excitement of living such a life and the terrible reality that no matter how hard I tried, I just couldn't attain the required standard. I resigned myself to accept that the life Jesus described here was for special people, a select elite who knew something I didn't. If these people existed, they didn't inhabit my world, and I'd certainly never inhabit theirs. However, I was also troubled: why would Jesus teach the Sermon on the Mount, knowing that we couldn't possibly achieve it? Why present a Masterplan for life, fully aware we would fail to live up to it? It didn't make any sense for him to talk about a life I couldn't live.

Gradually, while reading other parts of the New Testament, it dawned on me that I had been partially right all along - but for the wrong reason. Living the Christian life isn't difficult at all - it's impossible! God never intended his children to try and live up to his standard in our own strength. Christianity isn't us doing our best for God, struggling and straining as hard as we can to please him. There's only one person who can live the Christian life - Jesus Christ. Verses like these started to take on a new meaning for me:

I no longer live, but Christ lives in me. The life I now live in the flesh, I live by faith in the Son of God, who loved me and gave himself for me. (Galatians 2:20)

Since the Spirit of him who raised Jesus from the dead is living his life as God in you, then he who raised Christ from the dead will also bring your mortal bodies to life through his Spirit who lives his life as God in you. (Romans 8:11, author's translation)

If anyone is in Christ, there is a new creation; old things have passed away, all things have become new. (2Corinthians 5:17)

I had always thought being a Christian meant that God helped me live my life; but God doesn't do that. He takes away our old life and gives us a new one - his life. When I was born again into the kingdom of God the old Roger died and a new Roger came into being. This new Roger has the Holy Spirit living in me: and he has come to live the life of Jesus in me. Eventually, my entire life was revolutionised: instead of trying to live for God the best I could, I now knew that my responsibility as a Christian is to allow Jesus to live his life in me, through the Holy Spirit. Jesus promises that when the Holy Spirit comes to live in us we will receive power (Acts1:8). The New Testament word for power means *ability* (we get our English word dynamite from it). God the Father gives us the ability - the dynamic power - to live as his disciples by sending the Holy Spirit to live the life of Jesus in us. All the ability it took to create the universe is now living in us! The Ability is the Holy Spirit.

Inevitably my approach to the Sermon on the Mount subsequently changed dramatically. Instead of being overwhelmed by its impossibility, I now realised that in it Jesus presents his Masterplan to his disciples, fully aware that we are able to live this amazing life through him. Therefore, I no longer view the Sermon on the Mount as a target to aim at, knowing I'll never achieve it. Rather, I now understand it's the way of life for all Jesus' disciples, no matter who we are.

In the following chapters we're going to explore the Masterplan in detail together. I sincerely hope that you will be blessed, encouraged, challenged, and most of all, transformed by the incomparable words of Jesus.

ONE

WHAT IS THE SERMON ON THE MOUNT?

The Sermon on the Mount is the body of teaching given by Jesus at the beginning of his public ministry as recorded in Matthew chapters 5 to 7 (Luke has a shorter, parallel passage in Luke 6:17-49). The Sermon on the Mount follows on from Jesus' baptism, temptation in the desert, and calling of the first group of disciples. Matthew chapter 4 concludes with Jesus travelling around the region of Galilee in northern Israel, teaching and preaching the good news of God's kingdom, healing every sickness and disease he encountered, and liberating people from evil spirits. Not surprisingly, large crowds began to follow Jesus wherever he went, fascinated by him, drawn to his teaching and to the signs, wonders and miracles he performed. They had never encountered anything remotely like this before; Jesus' impact on them was incredible.

    Inevitably, Jesus grew in popularity and his fame rapidly spread like wildfire. If he'd so desired he could have ridden the wave of popular opinion to great effect, and caused a social and political revolution in the nation. In fact, this is exactly what many of those early followers expected: a powerful king like David who would restore the kingdom of Israel to its former glory and drive out the occupying Roman forces. But Jesus had another agenda: he came to establish another kind of kingdom - the kingdom of God. It's at this point of his growing popularity, in the early days of his emergence, that Jesus presents his kingdom manifesto, the Masterplan. He describes the life that his disciples, both his immediate followers and those throughout history, live in the power of the Holy Spirit.

    The Sermon on the Mount contains several phrases that have passed into everyday use, even by those who have little or no idea where they come from. They are used to encourage a certain kind of moral code or attitude: 'go the extra mile'; 'turn the other cheek'; 'the salt of the earth'; 'let your yes be yes'. It also contains some of the most famous words in the English language: what we call the

Lord's Prayer. The Sermon on the Mount is packed full of powerful, life-changing, radical teaching, all of which has Jesus' own practical application of how to live it. Our aim in this book is to unpack the Sermon on the Mount to show how we can successfully live this Masterplan.

A 'Sermon' on the Mount?

We call this passage in Matthew chapters 5 to 7 the Sermon on the Mount; however, that term never appears in the Word of God, which simply states that *Jesus began to teach them* (Matthew 5:2). It's a term that has grown into common use over the centuries and is now the accepted title of Jesus' teaching in this section of Matthew's Gospel. Personally, I think that is unfortunate; to call it a sermon could conjure up a certain, fixed idea in our minds. We must not approach the Sermon on the Mount with the mindset of listening to a sermon in the way we do in our church meetings. It's not a sermon in that sense at all. We don't listen to it, taking notes of the various points or considering its merits. We embrace it in its entirety as the normal life of Jesus' disciples. The Sermon on the Mount is not a proposition to be considered: it is a life to embrace.

We must also ask: to whom is Jesus presenting the Masterplan? The Word of God tells us that there were two groups of people in attendance - the crowds and his disciples. Jesus is primarily addressing his disciples, those who followed him, those he had called up to that time (there would be more of them later in his ministry). However, the crowds also heard his teaching, so in a very real sense it is addressed to them too. For the disciples, those who had already made their commitment to follow him, Jesus says: 'This is how you live.' For the crowds who are listening in, Jesus says: 'If you want to become one of my disciples, this is what it will mean for you.'

A disciple is a learner, a follower, a devoted adherent of somebody who is the disciple's Master. The purpose of discipleship is that the Master fashions the disciple, so the disciple becomes like the Master. The disciple embraces and adopts the life of the Master. Discipleship in the New Testament always involves a relationship. Many people had disciples: rabbis, the Pharisees and John the Baptist, for example. The major difference between Jesus and others who had disciples was that he chose his, whereas for others it was possible to apply to be their disciple. You could choose the Master you intended to follow and, in certain circumstances, you could decide how long you would be their disciple. Jesus never allowed that. It's true that many people followed him and some even attempted to become his disciple for their own reasons, but Jesus never accepted them, especially when they tried to put conditions on their discipleship (see Luke 9:57-62). Jesus called his own disciples with a simple command: 'Follow me', and unlike some other rabbis, he didn't seek merely to impart information or principles to them. He demanded a life-long commitment to himself. Whereas one could be a disciple for a season, Jesus said that if a person became his disciple, it was for life, and for every second of that life. He was prepared to give his life for his disciples: he expected the same commitment from them. The Sermon on the Mount, therefore, is the Master's plan in which he sets out in detail what he means when he calls us to be his life-long disciples.

All Christians are disciples (Acts 11:26); they are not limited to the pages and times of the New Testament. Disciples are not an elite band of believers. If you claim to be a Christian then you are a disciple of Jesus Christ; his Masterplan in Matthew 5 to 7 is for you.

Consider/Discuss
What is your favourite part of the Sermon on the Mount?

Jesus expects a life-long commitment to him from his disciples: have you made that commitment to him?

TWO

BLESSED: THE BEATITUDES

Blessed...blessed...blessed (Matthew 5:3-11)

Jesus begins the Masterplan with a simple, yet dynamic word: 'Blessed.' He repeats it eight times in the next few verses; therefore it must be a fundamental aspect of being his disciple. This first section of the Sermon is commonly called the Beatitudes, which is an old word to describe being supremely blessed. I've also heard it called the Beautiful-Attitudes, which is rather apt. The word *beatitude* is not in the actual text; nevertheless it is okay to use since it summarises what this section is all about: how to be blessed and how to be a blessing.

The word 'blessed' is one of those words often used without realising exactly what we are saying. Blessed, blessing and other forms of the word are used prolifically in both Old and New Testaments. The Hebrew word (*barak*) means *to kneel in adoration*; that's why it's often employed when we are exhorted to *'bless Yahweh'* (Psalm 103:1). It demonstrates the attitude we have when we praise and worship God (some translations use the word 'praise' instead of 'bless' to show this meaning). When it's used to show God blessing people or when we bless others it conveys a specific, determined attitude towards that person: that they will be *well, prosperous, successful*, and most of all, *happy*. It also means to *congratulate somebody* and *to rejoice with them in their success*. To be blessed means to live in this state of well-being with God and others.

Similarly, in the New Testament, the word blessed (*makarios*) means *to be happy, to be envied, well off, fortunate*. It means *to possess the favour of God and all his fulness*. It's no coincidence that when God created Adam and Eve, the first thing he did was bless them (Genesis 1:28). He intended that they should live forever in his fulness and favour. Tragically, Adam and Eve had other ideas. When God appeared to Abraham and called him to leave his homeland, he told him that he would bless him and make him a blessing to the whole earth (Genesis 12:1-3).

For disciples of Jesus, to be blessed primarily means that we are fully satisfied with knowing Jesus, with belonging to Jesus, with Jesus himself! Our complete satisfaction with the Lord Jesus alone means that our circumstances have no bearing on our state of blessedness. To be a blessed disciple of Jesus, therefore, is not a circumstantial happiness. Whatever happens to us - good, bad or ordinary - these things have no bearing on our blessedness at all. That state of being blessed then permeates out from us: we are a blessing to others because we are blessed. Since our well-being does not depend on what happens to us - or what doesn't happen to us - we constantly convey our total satisfaction with Jesus in all circumstances. We can't help it: because we are blessed we naturally bless others. That is why in the New Testament thankfulness and gratitude are often seen as evidence of blessing (Ephesians 1:3). When we bless others, through our words and actions, we pass on to them the blessing that we live in. Our lives have a tangible, beneficial effect on people. It also means we don't need to chase after other things to satisfy us. We will see how Jesus tackles this attitude when he talks about our priorities in seeking the kingdom of God rather than things (Matthew 6:33).

Jesus then breaks this blessedness into manageable pieces for us. He describes circumstances and attitudes that every disciple faces; in each one he explains that if we live in this state of blessedness there are tangible effects - on us and on others.

Here at the beginning of his teaching, Jesus addresses the heart of his disciples: are we satisfied with him alone, irrespective of favourable or unfavourable circumstances? If so, we are blessed and a blessing, and he regards us as his true disciples.

Consider/Discuss

In what ways has God blessed you, and how does he continue to bless you?

How do you practically bless God and others?

THREE

THE POOR IN SPIRIT

Blessed are the poor in spirit, because the kingdom of heaven belongs to them. (Matthew 5:3)

The first thing Jesus mentions in the Masterplan is the kingdom of heaven (Matthew's term for the kingdom of God). In the previous chapter we explored the true meaning of blessing; now Jesus explains the various ways his disciples are blessed. The first characteristic of a blessed disciple is to be poor in spirit. Before we discover what that means, let's state two things that it definitely is not.

First, to be poor in spirit doesn't mean to be materially or financially poor (even though Luke omits the phrase 'in spirit' in Luke 6:20 he means the same thing as in Matthew's account). The Bible does not teach that there is any spiritual benefit or value in poverty. Neither poverty nor wealth brings a person closer to God. Those who advocate a life of poverty as somehow an attainment of spiritual blessing are mistaken. The Bible certainly teaches the dangers of chasing wealth and the power of Mammon (the spiritual forces behind the love of money). It warns us that the love of money is a root of all kinds of evil (Matthew 6:24; 1Timothy 6:10), but it never advocates the pursuit or acceptance of poverty as a spiritual or blessed activity. Jesus was not poor: he was a skilled carpenter who would have made a good living from his craft. He had people who supported him financially in his ministry. Judas Iscariot was a thief who helped himself to the funds (John 12:6). We must also emphasise that having material wealth does not necessarily mean you're blessed. People get rich in many ways, honestly and dishonestly, through hard work and through illegal means.

Second, being poor in spirit doesn't mean that we should live as 'spiritual nobodies' - like those who delight to live in a poor spiritual state, limping along from crisis to crisis, displaying a downtrodden, weak 'I am nothing' Christianity. This kind of false spirituality conveys a nothingness that is not genuine, because it concentrates on the self. In fact, it's entirely self-centred. It's the hallmark of those who delight in their 'nothingness', who bear themselves around with a doleful countenance, who speak of their own insufficiency and inadequacy more than the greatness of the God they purport to serve and represent. This is nothing but pride in the guise of humility.

What, then, does it mean to be blessed by being poor in spirit? The answer lies in the phrase 'in spirit' and in the fact that Jesus refers to the kingdom of God. The nature of the kingdom is in the Holy Spirit (Romans 14:17); Jesus is the King of the kingdom. The kingdom is Jesus' righteousness, Jesus' peace and Jesus' joy; these are the hallmarks of the kingdom. When we are born again into the kingdom by the Holy Spirit (John 3:3-5), the Holy Spirit indwells us with the righteousness, peace and joy of Jesus. When the kingdom is established in us at our new birth, nothing of us remains; it is all of Jesus and nothing of us. Therefore, to be poor in spirit means the complete and utter emptying of ourselves. The Christian life is an exchanged life, not a changed life. For a disciple of Jesus, the way of blessing is quite simply to be empty of self: the kingdom of God deals a death blow to our self-righteousness, to our reliance on ourselves, and to our thinking that we can live this new life in our own strength through our own attainments. Realising that can either be a blessed relief or a major blow to our sense of self-importance.

In the Old Testament, when the exiles returned from their captivity in Babylon, God told their leader Zerubbabel to rebuild the temple. God gave him strict instructions: *'Not by might, nor by power, but my Spirit'* (Zechariah 4:6). Might and power here mean *human strength, efficiency, wealth, and ability.* God made it clear to Zerubbabel, as Jesus does to us in this passage: these natural things count for nothing in the kingdom of God. Only a complete reliance on the Spirit of God who lives that amazing life of Jesus in us means anything. Christianity is not a self-improvement programme. It is not about being the best you or an improved you; it is not about you and me at all. The New Testament puts it so powerfully when Jesus said, *'You can do nothing without me'* (John 15:5). Paul said the same thing many years later: *'I can do all things through Christ who strengthens me'* (Philippians 4:13).

To be poor in spirit is not a special state we work hard to attain; neither is it spiritual or material poverty. It is our status as blessed children of God. It is a fundamental expression of the kingdom of God. It is not false modesty or a pretend humility; it simply means every day we allow the Holy Spirit to express freely the righteousness, peace and joy of the Lord Jesus, without us getting in the way by drawing attention to ourselves, or by taking the glory reserved for God alone, or by behaving in such a manner that detracts from him in any way. After all, we are *his* disciples.

Consider/Discuss
Do you believe God wants to bless you materially?

What does it mean for you to possess Jesus' righteousness, peace and joy?

How liberating is it to know that Christianity is essentially all about Jesus and not about you?

FOUR

THOSE WHO MOURN

Blessed are those who mourn, because they will be comforted.
(Matthew 5:4)

This hallmark of Jesus' disciples is one that could possibly confuse us. How can those who mourn be blessed? How can a mourner be happy and fortunate? How does mourning display the favour and fulness of God? A wrong understanding of mourning might lead us to conclude that this characteristic encourages a kind of spiritual masochism, or that we should be miserable, depressed and constantly sad. Nothing could be further from the truth.

Jesus acknowledges that mourning is part of every disciple's life; we are not immune from the experiences of living in the world. It isn't wrong to mourn; in fact, we are told, *There is a time to mourn* (Ecclesiastes 3:4). Jesus also told us: *'You will have suffering in this world. Be courageous! I have conquered the world'* (John 16:33). The New Testament word for mourning means *to grieve, lament, have sorrow*, specifically *to grieve over a personal loss of hope through death or the end of something*. Mourning is an inevitable part of life for everyone, not only the disciple. Grieving the death of family members and close friends is normal and right. However, we should not confine mourning only to death. For Jesus' disciples there will be mourning over many things, including the impoverished condition of the church; the loss of brothers and sisters who fall away in their faith; friends who once walked closely in fellowship with us but who no longer wish to be associated with us in any way; the attitudes of leaders who care more about their positions and titles than the glory of God; the state of a world that persists in rejecting its Creator; friends who are martyred for their faith in Jesus; the abuse of the poor and downtrodden by the rich and powerful; the physical and sexual abuse of children; the neglect of the vulnerable; innocent people driven from their homes and countries by war; stateless refugees who languish in squalid camps because they have nowhere to go. Disciples have feelings; like our Master Jesus we are sometimes moved to tears and overcome with grief at the state of things and the pain and injustice that so many people suffer.

However, to mourn as a disciple is not to live in a permanent state of sadness, melancholy or depression, without any hope. God has made a wonderful promise to those who live in Zion - the church (see Hebrews 12:22-24):

> *The Spirit of Sovereign Yahweh is on Me, because Yahweh has anointed Me to...comfort all who mourn, to provide for those who mourn in Zion; to give them a crown of beauty instead of ashes, festive oil instead of mourning, and splendid clothes instead of despair. (Isaiah 61:1-3)*

There is the clue to how mourners are blessed - the anointing of the Holy Spirit. As is the case for so many of these Beatitudes the second part of Jesus' statement holds the key to understanding what he means: *those who mourn will be comforted.* The word here is *parakaleō*; students of New Testament Greek will immediately see the connection. Don't worry if you're not: I'll explain. This word is used widely in the New Testament; it means *to summon somebody to your side; to call on somebody to come to you to help you,* often as a legal representative to state your case. It is also translated as *exhort, urge, implore beseech, cheer, encourage and strengthen.* Most significantly, it is used to describe the Holy Spirit; he is described as the *Paraklētos*, the Comforter, Counsellor, Advocate (John 14:16-18; 15:26; 16:7). To be comforted in mourning is not to be wrapped in cotton wool or a security blanket, or to be cocooned within one's grief, no matter how raw and painful that grief might be. It is to receive the comfort, the strength, the healing, the overcoming ability of the Holy Spirit in one's time of mourning, that lifts us from the depths of despair and moves us forward in faith and hope. Remember: the kingdom of God is righteousness, peace - and joy - in the Holy Spirit. That is not an occasional experience; it is a permanent state of being for the disciple, no matter what situation one is experiencing. King David put it like this:

> *Even when I go through the darkest valley, I fear no danger; for you are with me; your rod and your staff - they comfort me. (Psalm 23:4)*

For the disciple who mourns there is blessing, strength and joy, even in the midst of that mourning. The Comforter not only sustains the mourner, he walks them through that season of mourning into the next without any residual bitterness, depression or emotional scars. He helps us so that during our mourning we are not only blessed, we are also able to be a blessing to others, to comfort and strengthen others who also mourn or suffer. Our mourning and the comfort of the Holy Spirit leads us to action - to comfort and help others with the comfort and help we receive. Paul encapsulated it like this:

> *Blessed be the God and Father of our Lord Jesus Christ, the Father of mercies and the God of all comfort. He comforts us in all our afflictions, so that we may be able to comfort those who are in any kind of affliction, through the comfort we ourselves receive from God. For as the sufferings of Christ overflow to us, so our comfort overflows through Christ. (2Corinthians 1:3-5)*

To mourn without the comfort of the Holy Spirit could lead us into all kinds and degrees of sadness and depression, or worse. When we mourn with the comfort of the Holy Spirit we know the blessing of God right in that situation and at the same time are able to comfort others who mourn, all because we have the Holy Spirit. Even in the darkest times of life we can still be blessed and be a blessing. That is remarkable; and an incredible testimony to the sustaining and overcoming power of the Holy Spirit.

Consider/Discuss
What causes you to mourn?

How has the Holy Spirit comforted you in your seasons of mourning?

Are there people who are mourning who need your comfort?

FIVE

THE MEEK

Blessed are the meek, because they will inherit the earth.
(Matthew 5:5)

If there is a Beatitude that is most misunderstood, I venture to say it's this one. This is demonstrated by the fact that Jesus has often been portrayed by certain Christian preachers, by film makers and artists as a timid, mild-mannered, emaciated, mystical figure, who looks like he is desperate for a good meal and in need of cheering up. This portrayal comes in part from a misunderstanding of meekness, where to be meek is to be weak, insipid and inoffensive. To be meek, Christians are told to be insignificant and almost devoid of personality, to be like doormats for others to walk over. The truth is that the meek are anything but that. Through their meekness Jesus' disciples inherit the earth.

The Greek word we translate as meek in this verse means *to demonstrate power without being harsh or cruel*. Meekness is the proper exercise of God's strength and power, while being under the control and direction of God. The meek exercise God's rule and authority humbly, in a God-like manner, as his representatives on earth. The meek, then, are truly authoritative. The meek *inherit the earth*: this takes us back to God's original intention for humanity to rule over the earth on his behalf (Genesis 1:26-28). Where Adam and Eve failed because of their sinful disobedience against God, the meek succeed because we have entered God's kingdom and humbly live under the authority of our heavenly Father, expressing and exercising his rule throughout the earth in every aspect of our lives. Paul uses similar language and this imagery of inheritance when describing who we are in Christ:

> *For you did not receive a spirit of slavery to fall back into fear, but you received the Spirit of adoption, by whom we cry out, 'Abba, Father!' The Spirit himself testifies together with our*

spirit that we are God's children, and if children, also heirs - heirs of God and co-heirs with Christ - seeing that we suffer with him so that we may also be glorified with him. (Romans 8:15-17)

Jesus described himself as meek: he said, *'I am meek and humble in heart'* (Matthew 11:29). The context of that saying describes him as also having great strength. He says to all who are weary and burdened: *'Come to me...you will find rest for your soul in me'*. Later in Matthew's Gospel, Jesus quotes the prophet Zechariah regarding himself as the Messianic King:

Your King is coming to you, meek, and mounted on a donkey, even on a colt, the foal of a beast of burden. (Matthew 21:5)

Meekness, therefore, is a quality of Jesus himself, and is demonstrated by the Holy Spirit through his disciples as we exercise his kingly rule here on earth. When we see Jesus in the Gospels we see a King full of the Holy Spirit, who walks in humility, yet with full confidence and great dignity. We see somebody who lives every day in the will of his Father, caring for the weak and helpless, the outcast and the underprivileged, who passionately cares about justice for all. We see somebody at home with rich and poor, high and low, who heals the sick, performs miracles, signs and wonders. We also see somebody who resolutely refuses to be pushed around by tyrannical religious powers, by the bullies of the political elite and by despotic Roman rulers. He is ruthless and withering in his attacks on all forms of hypocrisy. He expels from God's house of prayer those who had made it into a market. He calls stubborn, religious people 'children of the devil'. He lives contrary to the status quo of the earth's values and systems and resists all attempts to make him compromise his radical agenda of the kingdom of God. All this is meekness.

For Jesus' disciples, meekness is one of the most potent forces on earth. It's not being an overbearing bully, or trying to exercise one's will through the force of personality. It's not being a doormat for everybody to walk over, as we'll discover later in the Masterplan. It is the authority and power of God demonstrated through a humble spirit. The meek don't need to assert themselves or fight for their rights. By their very nature the meek are extremely dangerous, the best kind of dangerous, because they fearlessly challenge and confront everything that contradicts the kingdom of God. Since meekness is the expression of the strength of God, it also has all the authority and power of the Creator of the universe behind it. That's how the meek are enabled to inherit the earth. Those who decide to abuse, overpower or ridicule the meek are truly foolish and in considerable peril. They are taking on God himself; and they lose every time. The earth is the Lord's (Psalm 24:1) and he rules it through the meek; it's their inheritance. So don't mess with the meek.

Consider/Discuss

Has this chapter affected your understanding of meekness? If so, how?

As a meek person, how do you exercise the balance between living humbly under the control of God, and confronting what is contrary to the kingdom of God?

How do you respond when people try to walk over you, because they think Christians are doormats?

SIX

HUNGRY AND THIRSTY FOR RIGHTEOUSNESS

Blessed are those who hunger and thirst for righteousness, because they will be filled. (Matthew 5:6)

In this part of the Beatitudes, Jesus uses our God-given desire and need for food and drink to make his point. We get hungry and thirsty, so we eat and drink; and when we've had enough we're satisfied or full. Depending on who we are and where we live, and our appetite, we might do that two or three times a day. Whatever our eating and drinking habits, food and drink sustain us. They keep us alive and healthy - if we eat and drink the right things! It is often said that we are what we eat.

Jesus speaks here of a hunger and thirst for righteousness, a hunger and thirst that can only be satisfied by righteousness and by nothing else. Of course, he is referring to himself and that our hunger and thirst must ultimately be for him. He is our life, and we constantly feed from him, because we are always hungry for him. The Word of God describes Jesus as our righteousness: in the Old Testament he was prophetically called *Yahweh our Righteousness* (Jeremiah 23:6). In the New Testament he is called *the Righteous and Holy One* (Acts 3:14); and he was made sin for us so that in a glorious Divine exchange we become the righteousness of God in him (2Corinthians 5:21). The New Testament teaches that since we are the very righteousness of God - as holy as Jesus - from the moment of our new birth, we cannot become any more righteous. We are the righteousness of God in Christ now. Therefore, to be hungry and thirsty for righteousness doesn't mean we strive for more righteousness. We're already as righteous as we'll ever be.

Since Jesus is our righteousness, this hunger and thirst is primarily for him, to know him better, and constantly to grow closer to him. In a strange paradox we discover that while we are satisfied with Jesus, at the same time we want more of him! Paul expressed this constant hunger and thirst when he wrote: *I want to know him and the power of his resurrection* (Philippians 3:10). By this time Paul had been a Christian for more than 20 years and Philippians is one of his later letters. Yet he still had this hunger and thirst for Jesus; he wanted to know him better and more intimately. The Amplified Bible translates the verse like this:

For my determined purpose is that I may know him - that I may progressively become more deeply and intimately acquainted with him, perceiving and recognising and understanding the wonders of his Person more strongly and more clearly. (Philippians 3:10)

Just a note of caution here: we must be careful not to separate our righteousness from the One who makes us righteous. That is extremely dangerous and leads to legalism or self-righteousness, in which human pride rears its ugly head. Neither must we live in a constant struggle to attain what we already have: that will only lead to frustration and hopelessness.

Jesus said those who hunger and thirst for righteousness will be filled, they will be satisfied. Once you become hungry and thirsty for Jesus your righteousness, then you will be filled. You will not be smug or complacent, but satisfied with him alone. To hunger and thirst is not to strive for the unattainable, otherwise you will never be filled. It's not trying to reach an impossible standard of righteousness by your acts: it's resting (Paul describes it as 'sitting' in Ephesians 2:6-7) in who you are in Christ. It's a continuous process in which we know we have all of Jesus because the Holy Spirit lives in us; yet at the same time we want to know him even more.

This process of hunger and thirst, being full, hunger and thirst, being full, hunger and thirst, being full, means we are always maturing as disciples. The New Testament teaches that we grow in Christ increasingly until we reach the full stature and measure of the sons of God (Ephesians 4:11-13). But that process does not entail becoming more righteous: it means that we grow in who we already are as the Holy Spirit continues to conform us more and more into the image of the Son, as we grow from children of God to sons of God.

A hunger and thirst for righteousness will also cause us to be concerned with practical justice, with what is right. The Word of God often pairs righteousness and justice because righteousness and justice are the foundation of God's throne (Psalm 89:14). Therefore Jesus' disciples not only display his righteousness in our personal lives, we also demonstrate it by practically working for what is just - social, political, moral, economic. We express God's righteous justice in the various fields of work he leads us into, whether it's the world of finance, education, business, health care, politics, the arts, law, for example. God cares for the outcast and for those who suffer through injustice, in whichever way it manifests. Christians don't ignore all the injustices and unrighteousness in the world: we want to see people transformed from sinners to saints by the power of the Gospel of the kingdom. We also involve ourselves in establishing practical righteousness in our societies wherever we can. This regard for practical righteousness lay behind many of the great Christian social and political reformers like William Wilberforce (1759-1833), who successfully battled for the abolition of slavery. We must also mention the Christian philanthropist Elizabeth Fry (1780-1845), who campaigned for better conditions in Victorian prisons. She was known as 'the angel of prisons.' She also worked with the homeless and destitute. Both these saints changed the face of the societies they lived in, despite bitter and prolonged opposition. Many of the Old Testament prophets spoke passionately about justice. Amos prophesied to Israel when the nation was enjoying financial prosperity but ignoring the plight of the poor and needy. There was an appalling disparity between the haves and the have-nots. He warned them and proclaimed:

Let justice roll on like a river and righteousness like a never-failing stream. (Amos 5:24)

Jesus cares about the whole person; his kingdom is righteousness in the Holy Spirit. When we live righteously and seek justice in all its various expressions, we show that our hunger and thirst for righteousness is real, not merely theoretical.

Consider/Discuss

How do you maintain and increase your hunger and thirst for Jesus?

How do you practically express the righteousness of Jesus?

How concerned are you about practical justice in society?

SEVEN

THE MERCIFUL

Blessed are the merciful, because they will be shown mercy.
(Matthew 5:7)

So far in our exploration of Jesus' Masterplan we have discovered some aspects of the inner character of a disciple. Jesus now turns his attention to our disposition and behaviour towards others: we are merciful to them. There is much said in Christian circles today about love and grace, but love and grace without mercy are incomplete. Mercy is an aspect of God's love; together with his grace it is the way God exercises his love. Mercy and grace are the love of God in action:

Because of his great love for us, God, who is rich in mercy, made us alive with Christ even when we were dead in transgressions – it is by grace you have been saved. (Ephesians 2:4-5)

In him [Jesus] we have redemption through his blood, the forgiveness of sins, in accordance with the riches of God's grace that he lavished on us with all wisdom and understanding. (Ephesians 1:7-8)

Mercy and grace are two sides of the same coin. In showing us his loving mercy, God does not give us what we deserve: spiritual death, punishment for our sins, eternal separation from him in hell. Because God is rich in mercy, when we come to him and ask him for mercy, he gladly gives it, because he loves us so much. God has an unending supply of mercy for those who ask for it. That is the wonder of what Jesus has done in dying for us; he released the mercy of God. Asking God for mercy does not mean we have got away with anything; it's not a let-off. When we ask for mercy we are surrendering to the judgement of God. The fact that he loves us and wants to be merciful is beyond wonderful! Daniel understood God's mercy. When he prayed to God to begin the work of restoring God's people to their land, he appealed to God's mercy:

We do not make requests of you based on our righteous acts, but based on your great mercy. O Lord, listen! O Lord, forgive! O Lord, hear and act! (Daniel 9:18-19)

Take a moment to consider the enormity of God's mercy towards you, not only when you became a Christian but every day since. If you ever sin, he will always show you mercy if you ask him. Think of the number of times in your life when by rights you should have been punished for your disobedience to God. But you asked him to forgive you and have mercy on you. And he did; not reluctantly, but eagerly. That is real love. But there is more! God not only shows us his mercy, he also gives us his grace. In his mercy he does not give us what we deserve; but he goes further and also gives us what we do not deserve. We did not deserve forgiveness of our sins and the gift of righteousness: but that is precisely what he gave us. God is so generous that he lavishes his grace on us even though we do not deserve any of it.

Jesus says here that, like our heavenly Father, we too are merciful. Mercy and grace always display a generous, redemptive attitude to others; that's why mercy is such an important quality in the disciple. Our attitude to people is not judgemental or negatively critical. When somebody stands in genuine, humble need before us - if they are asking our forgiveness of their sins against us; appealing for our help because of their own stupidity or immaturity; asking for wisdom and guidance on their pilgrimage; prayer; a kind word; the list is endless - they make themselves vulnerable to us. This is a crucial moment for them; they put themselves at our mercy. They are saying: 'I need you; please help me.' In a very real way, at that moment we have genuine power: to show mercy, or to abuse, reject and turn the person away. Whenever anybody approached Jesus in this way he was always quick to show them mercy, without exception. At the same time he didn't allow people to get away with things. If they ever tried to justify their selfish actions, excuse themselves or fail to acknowledge their wrong attitudes, stupid mistakes or sinful behaviour, he always confronted them and told them straight. Mercy is not an excuse for sloppy, sinful living. Mercy is expressed when humility is expressed. And mercy itself is expressed humbly. The disciple who is meek, who is poor in spirit, who hungers and thirsts for righteousness, will always show mercy.

To the one who says, 'I can't do that,' or 'that's just unrealistic,' or 'I will try my best to attain to it,' the simple answer is: Jesus says it is the life of his disciple now. His Holy Spirit empowers us to live this way. If you are a disciple of Jesus, you are merciful.

Finally, this characteristic of the disciple also displays the law of sowing and reaping - we reap whatever we sow (Galatians 6:7.) This is a biblical law that runs right through the Word of God. It applies to everything concerning our lives, not only money - but it certainly includes that too. Jesus says that those who show mercy will themselves receive mercy; they will have the same humble attitude to God and others, acknowledging that they constantly live under the mercy of God and receiving mercy from others to the same measure they show it to others. The greater the measure of mercy we show will result in greater mercy being shown to us. Mercy, therefore, keeps us vulnerable and humble. It helps us handle power spiritually. It involves us in the lives of others in a spiritual dimension. Mercy teaches us value: the value of God's love, grace and holy righteousness, the value of our brothers and sisters in Christ, and the value of humility.

Consider/Discuss
How easily do you ask for mercy when you need it?

Is there anybody who needs you to show them mercy?

How does God feel when you show mercy to others?

EIGHT

THE PURE IN HEART

Blessed are the pure in heart, because they will see God.
(Matthew 5:8)

We have arrived at one of the most well-known sentences in the Masterplan. In this short statement Jesus addresses the core of discipleship - our hearts. There are hundreds of references to the heart in the Word of God. We don't have the space to mention them all here; I recommend that you get hold of a concordance or Bible dictionary and look them up for yourself. There are also many online Bible tools to help you.

In Scripture the heart describes the very centre of our being; it's a synonym for the inner being, for our spirit, our very identity. The heart is who we really are. Proverbs 4:23 warns us: *Guard your heart above all else, because it is the source of life.* The Word of God tells us that the heart of sinners is wicked, and the inclination of our heart is to sin (Genesis 6:5). That is why the great promise of God regarding the new covenant he would establish in Jesus Christ is so miraculous: *I will place my law within them and write it on their hearts. I will be their God and they will be my people* (Jeremiah 31:33.) This is the essence of the Gospel of the kingdom - in Christ we receive a new heart, a heart transplant, if you like. God doesn't merely give us a new set of laws to live by: he gives us a brand new life - a new heart.

The nature of our new heart in Christ is pure; Jesus says that his disciples have pure hearts. No wonder we are blessed! The Greek word for pure (*katharos*) is where we get our English word 'catharsis' from. It means *clean, unstained, upright, innocent, with no undesirable elements*. Catharsis means to purge something of anything bad or unclean, to make it clean and pure. That is what Jesus has done for us; he has purged our sin, removed our sinful nature, that evil heart, and replaced it with a new clean, pure heart.

Purity is another term for holiness and righteousness. The pure in heart are holy and righteous through Christ, therefore they will see God. Hebrews 12:14 states: *Pursue peace with everyone, and holiness - without it no one will see the Lord.* Our holiness before God (and the pursuit of peace, which we will explore later), enables us to 'see' God. We know that God is spirit and thus has no physical presence. The Word of God tells us that no-one can see God. We also discover in the Old Testament that sometimes God 'physically' appears to people: in human form, in a glory cloud, or with an overwhelming sense of his presence. Supremely and uniquely, Jesus, the Son of God, has fully revealed God to us: *If you have seen me you have seen the Father* (John 14:9.) Jesus also put a face on the Holy Spirit. Am I saying it's impossible for us to see God physically? I would not wish to be so presumptuous; God is sovereign and he can reveal himself in any way he chooses. The Word also tells us that one day we will see him as he is (1John 3:2.) However, Jesus has already brought God out to us where God can be seen. He has made God 'visible' if you like. The word translated 'see' here means *to perceive, discern, to experience*. The pure in heart 'see' God; as the Psalm says they taste and see that the Lord is good (Psalm 34:8.) To see God is to know him in a personal relationship. The beauty of Christianity is that we actually enter into an intimate relationship with God; he becomes our Father. God is no longer a remote figure or a stranger. We don't have to speculate about what he is like or depend on the testimony of others who have met him. We know him; and we spend the rest of our lives getting to know him better! We sometimes describe eternal life as having our sins forgiven and going to heaven. That is marvellously true. However, Jesus defined eternal life in terms of knowing God:

This is eternal life: that they may know you, the only true God, and the one you have sent - Jesus Christ. (John 17:3)

When God gave us eternal life he opened up the way for us to meet him and know him. Until we received our new, pure hearts that was impossible. But now we can genuinely say that we are in an eternal relationship with the God who made us. The blessedness of a disciple is that we have received a new, clean, pure heart, which has made us holy and righteous and brought us to a place where we know God personally. We are in the privileged position of being able to experience God, to see him and know him as he really is. Knowing God is the greatest thing that can happen to human beings: it's the reason why God created us. We love him with all our heart, with all that we are in our new nature in Christ; and we love our neighbour in exactly the same way. As we shall see in the next chapter, the natural lifestyle of pure-hearted disciples is to be makers of peace.

Consider/Discuss
What does it mean to you to be pure in heart?

What have you discovered about God that you didn't know before you met him?

How do you ensure your pure heart stays in good spiritual health?

NINE

THE MAKERS OF PEACE

Blessed are the makers of peace, because they will be called the sons of God. (Matthew 5:9)

This fallen world is constantly at war with itself. Every moment of every day, right across the globe, people are in conflict with each other, be it major conflagrations such as wars, ethnic vendettas, religious and political terrorism, antagonism in the workplace, boundary disagreements between neighbours or family feuds. Nation hates nation, race hates race, city hates city, town hates town, village hates village, neighbour hates neighbour, sibling hates sibling, children hate parents, parents hate children. The world is at war, and is destroying itself in the process.

This has been the condition of the world ever since Adam said no to God, and decided he could live without him. His own son, Cain, murdered his brother Abel, his own flesh and blood. War, hatred, conflict and disputes are all the result of Adam's refusal to live under the authority of God. He allowed sin to enter the world that he and Eve were supposed to rule on God's behalf.

Jesus calls his disciples the makers of peace (the only time this term is used in the New Testament). It is a remarkable description. The makers of peace, or peacemakers, are identified as God's sons, which itself is a major biblical image. In Isaiah's prophecy the coming Messiah will be the Prince of Peace (Isaiah 9:6); and the kingdom that Jesus established is righteousness, peace and joy in the Holy Spirit (Romans 14:17.) True peace is not the absence of war: it is first and foremost being at peace with God:
Since we have been declared righteous by faith, we have peace with God through our Lord Jesus Christ. (Romans 5:1)

To be God's peacemaker, one first of all has to be at peace with God - and that can only happen by being born again into the kingdom of God, thus becoming part of God's family. That's why the makers of peace are called sons of God: God is our Father and Jesus is our Lord and our elder brother (Hebrews 2:10-12). In a remarkable passage, Paul says that the entire creation is standing on tiptoe waiting for the manifestation of the sons of God (Romans 8:19). Our presence in this world has a positive effect on it; we represent the Prince of Peace, the God who created it.

Note that Jesus' disciples are *makers* of peace, we are not peacekeepers. There is a major difference between the two. We are not pacifiers or go-betweens. We are not those who merely act as barriers or human shields between enemies, like United Nations peacekeeping forces have to be. Through Christ we establish his peace; we don't keep the peace, we make the peace! The Gospel of the kingdom brings people into peace with God and with one another. That is important: some think that to be a peacemaker we must always compromise, or never make a fuss, and just be spiritual or political pacifists. But that is incorrect. We are not here to pour oil on troubled waters or to be so inoffensive that we become insipid. Somebody has defined this term peacemaker as *'those who bravely declare God's terms which make people whole.'* Peacemakers are God's instruments to bring his peace on his terms. That's a fundamental element of the Gospel of the kingdom. Therefore, they have to be prepared for conflict, opposition, abuse, even death, because natural man is at war with God. His sin makes him an enemy of God. In one of those seemingly paradoxical passages of the New Testament, Jesus said that the kingdom of God *'suffers violence and violent men take it by force'* (Matthew 11:12). Some versions translate this as *'the kingdom of God has been forcefully advancing and violent people have been forcing their way into it'*. Jesus is not advocating physical violence; we will see that later in the Masterplan. He is stressing the forceful nature of the kingdom, and how it 'violently' invades our lives to establish the peace of God. It also conveys the idea that, as Hebrews 12:28 says, we are always receiving the kingdom of God - we actively, continuously embrace the kingdom of God with all that we are. It's a constant attitude; we demonstrate a spiritual aggression to take the kingdom of God to ourselves. In doing so the kingdom of God advances and increases, bringing the peace of God. Peace with God comes only when the heart surrenders to its Conqueror and we receive his kingdom gladly, forcefully, into our lives. We lose and God wins!

Peacemakers are those who declare without fear or compromise the rule of God. Because they are righteous, meek, pure in heart and merciful, they respond to hatred with love, to violence with meekness, to conflict with peace. Later in the Masterplan we will see in greater detail how Jesus makes our being peacemakers practical. He will lay out in specific ways how we act towards our fellow disciples and to the world. For now we must understand that the best efforts of the United Nations, Truth and Reconciliation Commissions, arbitration committees and political legislation regarding hate and racist crimes, while to be applauded, will never deal with the fundamental issues that cause conflicts and wars. Only the Prince of Peace can ultimately solve that problem; and he has chosen his peacemakers to be the means of establishing his peace. That is why the most tragic and obscene spectacle is when Jesus' peacemakers declare war on each other: when Christians hate each other, separate from each other, take each other to court, gossip about each other. It is a denial of our very nature as God's sons. We are the makers of peace; so let us live in peace with each other (2Corinthians 13:11).

Consider/Discuss

What is the difference between a peace-maker and a peace-keeper?

Are there any situations that you currently need to bring the peace of God to?

TEN

THE PERSECUTED

Blessed are those who are persecuted for righteousness, because the kingdom of heaven is theirs. (Matthew 5:10)

Jesus' next Beatitude returns us to the first one, in that he mentions again the kingdom of heaven. This time he speaks of an inevitable consequence of being his disciple: persecution. The second century church leader Tertullian famously said, 'The blood of the martyrs is the seed of the church.' Church history is full of accounts of those millions of our brothers and sisters who bravely faced persecution in all its forms: their 'crime' was that they were Christians. Persecution of Christians is still rife today: hundreds of thousands suffer every day for their faith in Jesus Christ. In some parts of the world they are murdered by their own communities, even by their families. Church leaders are attacked, brutalised and beaten. Christians are driven from their homes and imprisoned or executed by their ungodly governments, which declare that Christianity is illegal. I have friends in certain countries who have been imprisoned simply because they are Christians. In other parts of the world, especially here in the west, Christians lose their jobs or experience discrimination because they refuse to follow anti-Christian unrighteous laws their governments pass. At the time of writing, a Christian preacher in the UK was recently compensated because he was taken into police custody and held without proper care, for saying publicly that homosexuality is a sin. As long as there are Christians there will be persecution.

The Word of God is clear, not only in this saying of Jesus, that persecution is part and parcel of being a disciple of Jesus. Elsewhere, Jesus said, *'The world hates me because I testify about it - that its deeds are evil'* (John 7:7). That is the fundamental reason why Christians are persecuted: Jesus' righteousness, and consequently that of his disciples, exposes the basic problem of the world - it is evil. Even though God loves the world, he hates what it has become in rejecting him. There is something about the fallen, sinful world that it always reacts against the righteousness of God. It cannot abide God's holy standard. God loves the world but the world hates God. Behind this hatred is the evil one - the devil, the ruler of this world (John 16:8-11). He hates God and he certainly doesn't like those who identify with God - Jesus' disciples. We have to understand that while we love sinners and reach out to them with the love of God, we also stand against the world and all its values. We are contrarians in the purest sense of the word. We live at odds with the world; we are in it but we are not part of it. Our righteousness in Christ exposes the sin of the world - and the world doesn't like it one bit. Just being who you are in Christ causes the world to have major problems with you. That's why Paul could say: *The world has been crucified to me through the cross, and I to the world* (Galatians 6:14).

Jesus promised us that the world will behave like this towards us. He said, *'If they persecuted me, they will also persecute you'* (John 15:20). Paul put it like this: *All those who want to live a godly life in Christ Jesus will be persecuted* (2Timothy 3:12). Of course, the ultimate target of the world's persecution is not us disciples - it is our Master. We are just the battleground; what the world really hates is the righteousness of Christ. That is why Jesus said we are happy if we we persecuted for the sake of righteousness - we are so identified with the Righteous One that hatred, opposition and persecution will come our way, in various forms. Now let me make it clear: we are not to go out of our way to provoke persecution so we can wear it as a martyr's badge. That kind of attitude is not befitting a Christian. The blessing is not in the persecution; the blessing is being in Christ and being identified with him as his follower. Neither are we to be so obnoxious in our attitudes and behaviour that we turn the world against us through our unrighteous acts. We don't provoke the world to hate us. We don't burn down mosques and abortion clinics, and kill people for their religious or political beliefs. We will see that Jesus gives his disciples a clear mandate regarding how we are to live in the world and how to relate to it. All Jesus is saying in this statement is that the disciple has to realise and accept that to be his follower means we cannot view life as a popularity contest. We are not here to tell the world that it is alright. As A.W. Tozer said: 'We are not diplomats but prophets, and our message is not a compromise but an ultimatum.'

The world without God is a world in deep trouble. We are as Christ in the world and to the world; and when the world turns on us it is just the way the sinful world always behaves towards God and his people. Understanding that fact is key in being a disciple.

Consider/Discuss

Have you experienced any form of persecution because you are a Christian?

What does it mean for you to know that the world will hate you for being Jesus' disciple?

ELEVEN

FOR MY SAKE

Blessed are you when they insult you and persecute you and falsely say every kind of evil against you because of me. Be glad and rejoice, because your reward is great in heaven. For that is how they persecuted the prophets who were before you. (Matthew 5:11-12)

'Blessed...be glad...rejoice.' Not words that one would usually expect to read in the context of being on the receiving end of insults, lies and persecution. Nevertheless, in his final Beatitude, Jesus says this is the way we respond when such things happen to us. Jesus never advocates a martyr complex or victim mentality for his followers; he expects us to display happiness and to always rejoice. Paul put it like this to a church who knew times of persecution: *Give thanks in all circumstances, for this is God's will for you in Christ Jesus* (1Thessalonians 5:18). The over-riding attitude, or the default setting, of the disciple is joy; it is the inevitable overflow of being in the kingdom of righteousness and peace in the Holy Spirit. As we have previously discovered, persecution, in all its guises, is part and parcel of being identified with the Lord Jesus Christ. The New Testament word for persecution used here means *to hunt down, to hound, to chase or put to flight*. We don't have to go looking for it; rest assured it will come in some form at some point in your life. When it does: rejoice, be glad, be blessed.

Jesus also speaks here about being insulted (the word means *to revile or to ridicule*). Later in the Masterplan he deals specifically with the ways people insult us; here he says when it happens, rejoice, be glad, be blessed. Many years after Jesus taught his Masterplan, Peter wrote: *If you are insulted for the name of Christ, you are blessed, because the Spirit of glory and of God rests on you* (1Peter 4:14). Remember: you are not the ultimate object of the insult - Christ is, and he's big enough to handle it.

Jesus also mentions those false accusations and lies that will inevitably come our way as disciples. Christians are often the targets of all kinds of evil lies and false rumours. I am not talking about the honest criticism that rightly comes our way if we are hypocritical or if we convey a false image of Jesus to the world. We are not immune from such accusations; unbelievers have the right to expect high standards from us. Here Jesus is tackling the fact that we have an enemy - Satan is a liar and the father of lies (John 8:44). He hates you, if you are a follower of Jesus. He will do all he can to defame and slander God; it's been that way since he deceived Eve in the Garden of Eden. Don't worry about that; just behave with integrity and believe in the integrity you have in Christ. Above all, believe in the integrity of God and his Word.

Jesus lifts the reason for persecution, insults and lies from us - he says it's all 'because of me.' Many times in the Gospels Jesus speaks like this. We find the phrases 'for my sake,' 'on account of me,' or as it is here: 'because of me' (see other examples in Matthew 10:22; John 15:21). When we decide to follow Jesus as his disciples, we become identified with him in every aspect of our being. We rightly make much of our being in Christ, being the righteousness of Christ, being as holy as Christ. We are like him. These are wonderful benefits. However, there is another side to that coin: everything we are and everything we do is 'because of him.' Our lives are so inextricably linked with Jesus; not only in our partaking of his righteousness and holiness, but also in bearing the hatred that the world has for him.

In it all, Jesus tells us two encouraging things. *First*, he says we have a great reward in heaven. Sometimes we interpret this as meaning when all our troubles are finished on earth, all will be peace and safety in heaven. That is true; but heaven is not an escape hatch from the world. There is an ultimate reward for each of us in heaven; but we enjoy the benefits of heaven now while we live on earth. The kingdom of God is here now. We are citizens of heaven now; we sit with Christ in the heavenly realms now (Ephesians 1:3; 2:6). We have the King of heaven living in us now through the Holy Spirit. We are over-comers now; we reign in life now. We're filled with peace and joy now. Life is wonderful now! We receive the rewards of heaven each day, not only when we die.

Second, Jesus reminds us that in times of persecution, insults and lies - and they are not necessarily constants in our experience - we are in good company. The Old Testament prophets knew the same; Isaiah, Jeremiah, Daniel, Amos, Elijah, Moses and the rest, all experienced it before us, and they all overcame. We are part of a great prophetic company of men and women, the great cloud of witnesses, who have gone before us. Our lives speak prophetically to this world, just as theirs did. Hebrews 11:38 says the world was not worthy of them - our forebears in the faith were too good for this sinful world. Yet none of them escaped from it; sometimes they even failed, they became discouraged and some suffered terribly. However by their faith in God every last one of them overcame. So do we. Take time to read Hebrews chapter 11; it will encourage you and spur you forwards. As you read you will meet many heroes of the faith there who have gone before you. They are cheering for you and urging you onwards and upwards!

When you become God's mouthpiece as his disciple, your life speaks volumes about your Master and Lord. So, don't be afraid: just let your life be the voice of God. You're in great company.

Consider/Discuss

What do you learn from the Old Testament prophets that encourages you in difficult times?

How do you practically appropriate and live in the good of your heavenly reward now?

TWELVE

THE SALT COVENANT

You are the salt of the earth. But if the salt should lose its taste, how can it be made salty? It's no longer good for anything but to be thrown out and trampled on by men. (Matthew 5:13)

Jesus introduces the next phase of his Masterplan with an affirmation and a warning. He affirms that his disciples are the salt of the earth; but if we fail to live up to that reality he warns us we are in danger of becoming useless to him.

'The salt of the earth' - what does that mean? For Jesus' initial hearers, the meaning was clear: the image of salt referred to enduring covenant loyalty. In biblical times, as it is today, salt was an integral part of daily life, used to flavour and preserve food. When people made covenants, they often ate meals together to ratify or confirm their covenant, and salt would always be present. Consequently, salt became intimately associated with covenant. We find this in the Word of God, where salt is often mentioned in regard to covenant. For example, every offering brought to God had to have salt added to it:

Season all your grain offerings with salt. Do not leave the salt of the covenant of your God out of your grain offerings; add salt to all your offerings. (Leviticus 2:13)

Because of salt's preserving qualities it was seen as a sign of endurance and permanence - an essential aspect of covenant. God himself directly instructed Aaron and the Levites:

Whatever is set aside from the holy offerings the Israelites present to Yahweh I give to you and your sons and daughters as your regular share. It is an everlasting covenant of salt before Yahweh for both you and your offspring. (Numbers 18:19)

The kings of Judah understood that God had made an everlasting covenant with David regarding his royal house. After the death of Solomon, Jeroboam rebelled against the kingdom. He was sharply reminded by David's descendant King Abijah:

Don't you know that Yahweh, the God of Israel, has given the kingship of Israel to David and his descendants forever by a covenant of salt? (2Chronicles 13:5)

When Jesus addressed his disciples as the salt of the earth, they immediately knew he was defining them as covenant people. That is who we are: we 'flavour' the earth with the covenant nature of God. God is not only a God who makes covenant: God *is* a covenant: he is one God in three Persons - the Father, the Son and the Spirit. Therefore, his disciples are covenant people. The church is a covenant community, and covenant is therefore a vital ingredient of the kingdom of God.

In fact, so vital is this aspect of covenant to our DNA as God's people that Jesus speaks in graphic terms about us: we dare not lose our 'saltiness'. We must not forsake or neglect our identity as God's covenant people. In Luke's account, this statement of Jesus is added: *'[the salt] isn't fit for the soil or the manure pile; they throw it out'* (Luke 14:35). Jesus says that those disciples who abandon, deny or live contrary to their covenant with their fellow disciples are useless to him. He can't use them for his purpose - not even 'for the soil or the manure pile' (as fertiliser). The warning is evident: no matter what activity we give ourselves to in Jesus' name, if we are not living in covenant with each other as his disciples, Jesus in effect says: 'You're not fit for purpose, I don't have any use for you, I don't know what to do with you. You're not my disciple.' I never want to hear him say that to me: do you?

Our modern understanding of salt could negatively impact the power of Jesus' statement on us: how can salt become tasteless? Our salt is processed and keeps its flavour; but the salt of Jesus' time didn't benefit from our modern production techniques. Salt was produced with other remaining ingredients in it; if the salt was left to the elements - to vapour or dilution - it would evaporate and only the impurities or gritty minerals would remain. The 'salt' would be therefore useless, tasteless. Once we neglect covenant then all that's left is tasteless grit; it might look fine and acceptable to us, but it's no longer the salt that flavours the earth with the covenant of God.

In Mark's Gospel Jesus says: *'Everyone will be salted with fire...have salt in yourselves and be at peace with each other'* (Mark 9:49-50). Fire purifies; it burns up and removes things. The image of fire is sometimes used in the Word of God to show the proving or testing of something. That's what Jesus means here. He says that our claims to be God's covenant people are inevitably tested to prove how genuine we are. That means for each one of us as Jesus' disciples we must have salt in ourselves: we are a covenant man or woman in reality not theory. The evidence of that is we live at peace with each other. Every time the Body of Christ divides or tears itself, we deny not only who we are - covenant people - we also deny who God is. That's why Jesus' warning to us is so alarming; it deals a death blow to the individualist and the independent, to the selfishly ambitious and the isolationist, to the divisive and the gossip, to the one who swears unfailing loyalty then walks away from his brothers and sisters to further his own ends. To all our activities, the Holy Spirit holds up before us the salt of the covenant - the fundamental ingredient in all that we are.

Consider/Discuss

What does it mean for you to be part of God's covenant people?

How do you express your covenant to your fellow disciples?

What should our attitudes be towards those Christians who don't want to live as part of the covenant community?

THIRTEEN

LIGHT OF THE WORLD

You are the light of the world. A city situated on a hill cannot be hidden. No one lights a lamp and puts it under a basket, but rather on a lamp-stand, and it gives light for all who are in the house. In the same way, let your light shine before men, so that they may see your good works and give glory to your Father in heaven. (Matthew 5:14-16)

When Jesus spoke again to the people, he said, "I am the light of the world. Whoever follows me will never walk in darkness, but will have the light of life." (John 8:12)

Jesus' next description of his disciples intimately identifies us with him: 'I am the light of the world: you are the light of the world.' In case you feel like shying away from such a remarkable comparison, remember that it is Jesus who defines us, and surely that is good enough. As the Word states elsewhere: ...*We are as he is in this world* (1John 4:17). Isn't it fantastic to be defined by Jesus in such a way! I love the fact that Jesus isn't ashamed to be associated with us; obviously he has a high regard for his followers.

Of course, we are not Jesus Christ; that isn't what Jesus means. He is the unique Son of God; let's be clear about that. Nevertheless, Jesus says that we are just like him, which is an essential aspect of Christianity. Christians are not forgiven sinners; the blood of Jesus has made us righteous saints. Jesus calls himself and us the light of the world; that's fascinating because the first thing God created was light (Genesis 1:3). Since we know that the creation speaks of the nature of God (Psalm 19:1-4), we should expect the first thing he created to reveal something fundamental about him. That is why the Word also says: *Now this is the message we have heard from Him and declare to you: God is light, and there is absolutely no darkness in Him* (1John 1:5). Taking up that creation passage, and deliberately using the phrase 'In the beginning', John describes the incarnation of Jesus in terms of light: *The true light, who gives light to everyone, was coming into the world* (John 1:9). That is why we who are in Christ are described in terms of light: *For you were once darkness, but now you are light in the Lord. Walk as children of light* (Ephesians 5:8). Notice that - we *are* light in the Lord. Christian life is not sinners desperately trying to grope their way out of darkness towards something. We walk in the light because we *are* light; Jesus lives his life of light now in us. When Jesus says 'Let your light shine', he means, 'Let me live my life through you.' Let's say a couple of things about light:

First, light is highly visible. Consequently light is prominent. That is why Jesus speaks about us being like a city on a hill and putting a light on a lamp stand. The church is God's heavenly city on earth, full of God's kingdom people through whom Jesus shines with the light of his life. If you want to see what Jesus is like look at his church. To be a disciple means you will live prominently in your world. You are on display, naturally demonstrating and revealing Jesus. All that Jesus has spoken of in the Beatitudes is meant to be lived out in the public eye, among the people we live and work with: *'let your light shine before men, so that they may see your good works and give glory to your Father in heaven'* (verse 16). In a very real way, when people see us they see Jesus; they discover what he is like by looking at us. Jesus said a similar thing when he affirmed: *'If you have seen me you have seen the Father'* (John 14:9). If you like, Jesus made the invisible God visible. Let me reiterate: we are not God or gods in any way; but we reveal him because he lives in us.

Second, light guides and reveals. Have you ever tried walking in the dark with no street lights or the light of the moon to see by? I'm sure you'd never try and drive a car at night without your headlights on would you? Besides being illegal it's also extremely unwise. As the light of the world we guide people to Jesus - we could even say we show the way to the Way. Jesus is the Way, the Truth and the Life (John 14:6); many people find him by engaging with him through his disciples. I enjoy hearing the stories of people who have become Christians; often they tell how they encountered Jesus through one disciple or several. Each of these disciples guided them to Jesus, in all kinds of ways. I'm always encouraged by these stories; they show that Jesus is shining with his life in my brothers and sisters to guide people to himself.

Jesus tells us that our good works cause people to give glory to our Father in heaven. What are 'good works?' The answer is found in John 14:12 where Jesus says: *'I assure you: The one who believes in me will also do the works that I do. And he will do even greater works than these, because I am going to the Father.'* Jesus continues to live on earth by the Holy Spirit and do all that he did when physically present only on a greater scale, through his disciples. I used to be intimidated by these words of Jesus: how could I do the same works - and greater works? The answer is simple: because he says so. The reason we do the same and greater works is because Jesus is doing them in us through the Holy Spirit. When Jesus was physically on earth he was 'confined' to one place at one time. If he was in Nazareth and you needed him you had to go to Nazareth. Today it's different. Jesus has gone global, so to speak! He is doing all the things he did when on earth on a greater scale because he lives in his disciples all over the world. We don't do greater works than Jesus - it's not a competition in which he fed five thousand so we feed ten thousand! It just means that the same power that raised Jesus from the dead is now in us, and just as people were awestruck by Jesus and gave glory to God constantly in the Gospels, so it is today. Jesus continues to fill the earth with the glory of God the Father through each and every disciple who owns the name of Jesus as their Lord. When we come to the Lord's Prayer we will return to another aspect of this terrific reality: we will discover that Jesus teaches us to pray about the glory of our Father.

Consider/Discuss

What do you think about being so intimately identified with Jesus as the light of the world?

In what practical ways is your life prominent as part of the city on a hill and the light on the lamp-stand?

FOURTEEN

TURNING POINT

Don't assume that I came to destroy the Law or the Prophets. I did not come to destroy but to fulfil. For I assure you: Until heaven and earth pass away, not the smallest letter or one stroke of a letter will pass from the law until all things are accomplished. Therefore, whoever breaks one of the least of these commands and teaches people to do so will be called least in the kingdom of heaven. But whoever practises and teaches these commands will be called great in the kingdom of heaven. For I tell you, unless your righteousness surpasses that of the scribes and Pharisees, you will never enter the kingdom of heaven. (Matthew 5:17-20)

We have reached a turning point in the Sermon on the Mount. Thus far, Jesus has been setting out several principles of the Masterplan. Next he takes us to the Old Testament Scriptures to put flesh on the bones of that plan. In order to do that he establishes his own relationship to the Word of God in general and the Law of Moses in particular. Jesus is the Word (John 1:1), the incarnate Word of God. Scripture is the breathed-out Word of God written down (2Timothy 3:16-17). There is no other Jesus but the one revealed in the Word of God; and the Word of God can only be understood from a personal relationship with the Jesus of the Word of God. If we always keep these two inter-related truths together we'll have a solid base on which we can build our faith.

Jesus begins this transitional stage with a statement intended to dispel any misunderstanding: 'In what I'm about to say I'm not destroying the Word of God' ('Law and Prophets' refers to the Old Testament as a whole). Jesus would never destroy or contradict his own word: if he did such a thing then everything would cease to exist - including him. Hebrews 1:3 tells us that he *'upholds the universe by his powerful word'*. We can trust God and his word completely;

that's why we are able to say that the Word of God is God's integrity.

Jesus says that he has come to fulfil the Word of God. Then he refers to the law of Moses, which had come directly to Moses from God at Sinai. Jesus affirms its divine origin, authority and relevance (*'until heaven and earth pass away...until all things are accomplished'*). That word 'accomplished' is a common New Testament word and means everything God planned and purposed in eternity being manifested and fulfilled in time-space history. It is beyond our scope to go into detail regarding the nature and function of the Old Testament Law. However, what we should note is that in the following verses Jesus makes reference to six passages from the Law of Moses with the phrase, *'You have heard it was said...but I tell you.'* Jesus, as the God who met Moses on Sinai, tells us: 'This is the true meaning of what I told Moses at Sinai.'

In the new covenant in Christ, the Law of God is 'internalised' within us by the Holy Spirit. In the Masterplan, Jesus takes the Law and gives it its original, eternal meaning. He takes us to the heart of the Law and then applies it to our everyday lives. He says, 'This is what it means to be my disciple seven days a week.' Far from merely repeating what was written, he asserts: 'This is what I meant in the 10 Commandments, and this is my ultimate intention for those words that I wrote on stone.' For example, he says in Matthew 5:21-22:

'You have heard that it was said to the people long ago, Do not murder, and anyone who murders will be subject to judgment. But I tell you that anyone who is angry with his brother will be subject to judgment.'

Jesus takes the Commandment and gives it its intended meaning and practical application to the new creation in Christ. Jesus is not contradicting the Law: rather, he reaches into the heart of the Law. God knew that one day the Law would be written on the hearts of his children. The great promise of God in the new covenant that Jeremiah spoke about several hundred years before Jesus was born, was that God would make a new covenant with us:

I will place my Law within them and write it on their hearts. I will be their God and they will be my people. (Jeremiah 31:33)

This is what Jesus achieved in his death and resurrection; he inaugurated a new way of living. He established the kingdom of righteousness, peace and joy in the Holy Spirit. Hence his instructions at the close of this section regarding righteousness: the scribes and Pharisees were notorious for flaunting their self-righteousness in front of everybody. They boasted that they were the guardians and interpreters of the Law (they even added another six hundred of their own rules to it). In the Gospels Jesus often clashed with them and he constantly warned the people about them. Here he prepares his disciples for what follows in the Masterplan: 'Don't get your sense of righteousness from the scribes and Pharisees; don't compare yourselves with them. Don't try and outdo them by being more self-righteous than they are. They are not to be your role models.' Jesus means that the standard of righteousness is not that of the scribes and Pharisees: the only righteousness that surpasses them is a different standard or kind of righteousness altogether. The standard is the Righteous One, the one who keeps the Law and fulfils it - Jesus himself. His disciples are just like him - righteous - because they have entered his righteous kingdom and now they have become the righteousness of Christ himself.

Consider/Discuss
How highly did Jesus regard the Old Testament?

How does your righteousness surpass that of the scribes and Pharisees?

What is a Christian's relationship to the Old Testament?

FIFTEEN

'I COULD KILL YOU'

You have heard that it was said to our ancestors, Do not murder, and whoever murders will be subject to judgement. But I tell you, everyone who is angry with his brother will be subject to judgement. And whoever says to his brother, 'Fool!' will be subject to the Sanhedrin. But whoever says, 'You moron!' will be subject to hellfire. So if you are offering your gift on the altar, and there you remember that your brother has something against you, leave your gift in front of the altar. First, go and be reconciled with your brother and then come and offer your gift. Reach a settlement quickly with your adversary while you're on the way with him, or your adversary will hand you over to the judge, the judge to the officer and you will be thrown into prison. I assure you: You will never get out of there until you have paid the last penny! (Matthew 5:21-26)

Jesus begins to explain and internalise the Law with a reference to the 10 Commandments: *'Do not murder'* (Exodus 20:13). Note that the Commandment does not say, *Do not kill*; it says *do not murder*. Why do we need to stress this? In the Word of God there is a difference between killing and murdering. The Law emphasised the difference, as do other Old Testament passages. For example: we see God himself putting evil people to death: Korah, Dathan and Abiram (Numbers 16); Er and Onan (Genesis 38:7-10). We are told: *there is a time to kill* (Ecclesiastes 3:3). No one in their right mind would charge God with murder. Furthermore, if the Law forbids killing then God has failed to keep his own Law. We might say that is the Old Testament, things are different in the New Testament. However, we see in the case of Ananias and Sapphira in Acts chapter 5, that it was God who took their lives: he killed them. And in Acts chapter 12, Herod was struck down by an angel of God and died. God was the instigator of these three deaths.

I am trying to tread carefully here; I don't want to misrepresent God in any way, nor do I wish to devalue the sanctity of human life. God is not a cold-blooded murderer; he doesn't commit random or calculated acts of violence. He is good, and everything he does is good (Psalm 119:68). Nevertheless, the Word of God says that God gives life, and he takes life away (1Samuel 2:6). If we see the difference that the Bible makes between killing and murder, we will appreciate even more the power of what Jesus is teaching us.

Murder is the worst kind of criminal act and the ultimate expression of hatred. Jesus takes us back beyond the Law to the first murderer, even though he doesn't mention him by name. Cain was the first murderer (Genesis 4:1-8); he murdered his own brother, Abel. Cain hated his brother because he was jealous of him. His hatred and jealousy became so much part of Cain that he attacked and murdered his own brother, the son of his father and mother, the man who had the same DNA as him. In murdering his brother, something also died in Cain. This hatred and jealousy ate Cain away like a cancer to the extent that he no longer valued or loved his brother. Cain lost all sense of reality and reason towards Abel; his heart became angry with his brother. So he murdered him. That hatred didn't blow up in a moment; it festered in Cain's heart, eating him away, distorting his mind, affecting the way he thought about his brother and the way he spoke to him. He had already murdered Abel in his heart long before he struck the fatal blow.

Jesus addresses the way we relate to our 'brothers' - a key New Testament term for the way the early believers saw themselves and a reminder that we are our brother's keeper (Genesis 4:9). This word 'brother' was used far more than any other term by the early New Testament church to describe their common identity and relationship to each other. They saw themselves as a family. In those days the term 'brother' was used to described both men and women when they were gathered together in mixed company (more modern translations of the New Testament use the phrase 'brothers and sisters').

Jesus warns us not to be angry towards our brother or sister in Christ. He doesn't say don't get angry: he says don't get angry with your brother. Jesus got angry: the same word is used in Mark 3:5 to demonstrate his own anger at the Pharisees. The difference here was that Jesus was angry and grieved by their stubbornness and hard hearts, by their arrogant unbelief and callous indifference to the plight of a sick man. That's a completely different expression of anger from what Jesus means here. He says, 'Don't hate your brother; don't get bitter and twisted towards your brother.' Jesus then explains how anger towards a brother expresses itself. Whatever our heart attitude to each other is, it will be evident in the way we speak to one another and about one another. The two words he uses to describe such anger - *Raca* and *Moros* - are extremely insulting (our word moron comes from *moros*). They are both expressions of sheer contempt, deliberately meant to provoke and demean others. They have a cruel and vindictive edge to them. That's why Jesus refers to judgement with regard to the way we speak and what we say: the Sanhedrin (the Ruling Council), prison, and the ultimate judgement - hell. It's a serious matter to treat your brother like this. Jesus uses the illustration of two adversaries who refuse to be reconciled: prison awaits and there's no way out until you pay the fine and the debt. The Sanhedrin had the power of life and death - they convicted Jesus at his trial. And hell is the final judgement for the sinner: there's no appeal court. In using these examples Jesus highlights the consequences of our actions if we hate our brothers and sisters; if we speak badly to each other and about each other. Rest assured: we won't get away with it and eventually we will have to face the consequences. Elsewhere in Matthew's Gospel Jesus returns to this theme, when he says that what we allow into our hearts will come out in our words: *'The mouth speaks from the overflow of the heart'* (Matthew 12:34). He assures us that on Judgement Day we will have to give an account not only for our actions but also for the words we have spoken:

> *I tell you that on the day of judgement people will have to account for every careless word they speak. For by your words you will be acquitted, and by your words you will be condemned. (Matthew 12:36-37)*

Jesus doesn't ignore the fact that brothers and sisters in Christ sometimes disagree and face conflict. He is a realist. That's why he provides a remedy and tells us how to resolve such conflicts - that we must nip them in the bud. In verse 23 Jesus gives us the solution: if you are worshipping the Lord and remember your brother has an issue with you, stop what you're doing and go to him. He's not talking about being in a meeting while you're singing songs - although that could happen. Since our whole life is worship we should be acutely aware at any time if things are not right between us and our brother. When you realise something is wrong - act straight away. You are always obliged to take the initiative in restoration. In going to your brother don't go to 'have it out' or to 'sort your brother out' or 'point out your brother's problem'. Jesus says, 'Go to your brother with one purpose - to be reconciled to him.' Jesus doesn't apportion blame, only responsibility. You should know your brother so well that you know when he's out of sorts with you or has a problem with you - whatever the cause or fault - yours or your brother's. It doesn't matter; go to him and be reconciled. Let's call to mind what Jesus has already taught us - be a maker of peace with your brother. Be quick to reconcile; settle differences swiftly; have a redemptive attitude; do all you can to win your brother. Why? Because he's your brother; you have the same Father; you share the same elder brother in Jesus; you're both sons of God. So live accordingly.

Consider/Discuss

Do you understand the biblical difference between killing and murder?

Why do people get jealous of others?

What does Jesus' teaching tell you about the importance of speaking properly?

SIXTEEN

I ONLY HAVE EYES FOR YOU

You have heard it was said, Do not commit adultery. But I tell you, everyone who looks at a woman to lust for her has already committed adultery in his heart. If your right eye causes you to sin, gouge it out and throw it away. For it is better that you lose one of the parts of your body than for your whole body to be thrown into hell. And if your right hand causes you to sin, cut it off and throw it away. For it is better that you lose one of the parts of your body than for your whole body to go into hell! (Matthew 5:27-30)

Jesus is interested in every aspect of our lives, including our personal morality. Here he instructs us regarding our sexual purity. Jesus makes a direct reference to the seventh commandment - do not commit adultery - and applies it to our hearts. As far as Jesus is concerned, adultery is not merely a physical act: the improper way of behaving toward the opposite sex in the way we look at each other and think about each other can itself be adulterous. This is truly radical: for Jesus a person can be adulterous in their heart without ever acting on that desire physically. This demonstrates yet again the importance that Jesus places on our inner being, our hearts, and the fact that ultimately only he can live this life. The good news is that's exactly what he does in giving us the Holy Spirit.

The word 'lust' here is a widely used New Testament term; it occurs in both a positive and negative sense. It means *to have a focussed passion, an intense, prolonged desire, to set one's heart on something in a determined fashion*. Jesus used it of himself in Luke 22:15 when he said to his disciples: *'I have **fervently desired** to eat this Passover with you before I suffer.'* It is also used to describe the enmity between the flesh (that behaviour in believers who are not under the control of the Holy Spirit, described in Galatians 5:19-21), and the Spirit:

> *The flesh **desires** what is against the Spirit and the Spirit **desires** what is against the flesh: these are opposed to each other. (Galatians 5:17)*

Jesus warns us against entertaining dangerous, immoral thoughts, especially since the next topic he will speak about is marriage and divorce. He is radical in his teaching - there is such power in lust, a wrongful, intense prolonged sexual desire towards somebody of the opposite sex, that it can destroy the disciple. So Jesus uses hyperbole to shock us - *'pluck your eye out...cut off your hand'* (verses 29-30). Jesus isn't being literal; he does not command self-mutilation as the cure for lust. You still have another eye and hand with which you can continue to lust! The point Jesus makes here is not to lust at all, and he uses intense imagery to get his message across. He says, 'Don't play with fire, or you'll get burned; don't be controlled by the flesh. Guard your heart by being controlled by the Holy Spirit'. To drive his point home Jesus purposely mentions the reality of Hell (verse 29-30) - there are eternal consequences to our actions in this life. Hell is real because the Word of God says it is. What's more, Jesus talked about it more than anybody else.

Practically, what does this mean for us as Jesus' disciples? This teaching on sexual purity applies to all believers: men and women, marrieds and singles, widows and widowers. We are all sexual beings; it's the way God made us. Sex is the creation of God and is good and beautiful; he just wants us to behave sexually and in all our morals the way he plans. I am married: therefore that will determine how I behave towards my wife and every other lady. Job 31:1 says, *I have made a covenant with my eyes. How then could I look at a young woman?* I do not walk around with my eyes closed; I can see other ladies. Adverts and images appear before me everywhere, in public places, in newspapers and magazines; in movies and on television. Some of these images are deliberately designed to be sexual, let's face it. I have worked in the same offices as ladies, interacting with them as colleagues. My wife and I have friends who are ladies. But I have eyes only for my wife. Part of my marriage covenant with her is to be faithful to her for as long as we both live. That includes my sexual behaviour.

Jesus does not demand segregation of the sexes; rather, he instructs us how to behave properly towards each other as sexual and moral people. Don't let what you see get beyond your eyes into your heart; don't dwell on it and let it become a fixation - a lust. Don't entertain it: turn off the programme, stay away from pornographic websites, look away from that billboard, leave the room, avoid being alone with a lady in a compromising situation. Don't become fixated on another lady. The list of practical steps is endless. Of course, I speak as a man; for ladies the same is true. You might need to get help; make yourself accountable to spiritual people - your leaders or friends. Take positive action; 'gouge out your eye' or 'cut off your hand' by tackling the problem head on and living free.

The major thing is to live in fellowship with the Holy Spirit. Let him be your eyes; see things his way, let him fill you with Jesus' morality. Always remember that Jesus was a real man who had genuine feelings. He was like us in every way - even sexually. He faced all the things we face; he saw all the things we see; he knew ladies such as Mary and Martha as friends and always behaved properly towards them. One of his most devoted followers was Mary Magdalene, who had been a prostitute before she met him. The Bible says that Jesus was tempted in every way we are (Hebrews 4:15); but he never sinned. Jesus never allowed lust to control him; he was filled with the Holy Spirit and always made the right choices. If he could live morally free and sexually pure then so can we.

Consider/Discuss
How do you practically protect your moral eyes and heart?

Does it help you to know that Jesus was just like us morally and sexually, that he faced all the things we face?

SEVENTEEN

MARRIAGE AND DIVORCE

It has been said, 'Anyone who divorces his wife must give her a certificate of divorce.' But I tell you that anyone who divorces his wife, except for sexual immorality, makes her the victim of adultery, and anyone who marries a divorced woman commits adultery. (Matthew 5:31-32)

As I approach this part of Jesus' Masterplan I am acutely aware that I must be as sensitive as possible. The matter of marriage and divorce is one that touches many families: my own wider family has experienced several divorces. Each one has been incredibly painful and damaging to those involved, including their children. Therefore, in this chapter I intend to confine myself to the principles that Jesus outlines here regarding marriage and divorce. I know that once this important subject is raised a million-and-one questions might be asked about individual examples and hypothetical situations. Those will have to wait for a future occasion. For now, let me make the following observations on the passage.

First: marriage is God's great idea; it comes from within his very being. God loves marriage; he created it and performed the first marriage ceremony between Adam and Eve (Genesis 1:26-28; 2:18-25). As a result of Adam's covenant vow that Eve was now 'bone of my bone and flesh of my flesh' the Word of God says something that is repeated several times in the rest of the Bible - *for this reason a man leaves his father and mother and is united to his wife and they become one flesh* (see Ephesians 5:21-32; 1Corinthians 6:16). Jesus also uses this statement to define marriage (Matthew 19:1-8). Everything God creates reveals something about him, and marriage is no exception. Marriage demonstrates the oneness and distinctions of the Trinity (one God in three Persons); it describes the relationship between God and his people, and between Jesus and the Church. Marriage is just the way God is! He did it this way because that's the way he wanted. The fact that the Word of God begins and ends with a marriage is also highly significant (Revelation 21:9). Marriage is the 'God factor' in every society. We should also stress that by marriage we mean a covenant between a man and a woman; that alone is marriage. The Word of God never recognises so called 'same-sex marriages' and it always condemns homosexuality as sin. Governments and societies might legalise such things, but in God's sight they are not marriages at all. As far as God is concerned, marriage is confined to a covenant between a man and a woman. We should not be surprised at the current assault on marriage in our time; ultimately it is an assault on the character and nature of God.

Marriage is a lifelong covenant between a man and a woman. In their covenant vows and subsequent physical union their marriage represents God - even marriage between non-Christians does this. God is for all marriage, not only those of his children. In his teaching here, Jesus affirms the eternal principle and value of marriage. I am happy to report that marriage is here to stay.

Second: God hates divorce. This is where sensitivity is necessary. The Word of God is categorical that divorce is anathema to God: *'I hate divorce,' says Yahweh, 'because the man who divorces his wife covers his garment with violence'* (Malachi 2:16). There is no getting around this statement by God: divorce is grievous to him. He hates it because of what it does: it is a denial of his nature, it is the breaking of covenant, it sullies the image of Jesus and his bride. It also rips people apart; it tears lives to pieces; it damages children; it weakens society; it devalues God and the pinnacle of his creation - humanity. This is different from a marriage that ends in death: here a covenant has been fulfilled and completed. I remember when my father died; he and mum were married for forty years. She was devastated when he passed away, but her comfort was that they had lived together in covenant all those years. Interestingly, Jesus says that divorce is an option in certain circumstances; we even find provision for it in the Old Testament law - the certificate of divorce that Jesus refers to here. Divorce was a last resort, when every other option had failed. Later in Matthew's account, Jesus goes further into the matter of divorce, and why God allowed it: *'Moses permitted you to divorce your wives because your hearts were hard'* (Matthew 19:8). There is the reason - like everything else Jesus is tackling in the Masterplan, he is concerned with our hearts. He says divorce happens because something goes wrong in the heart. Let me say this: God hates divorce, he does not hate divorced people. I cannot emphasis that too much. God hates divorce because of what it does and because it reveals that a heart has gone wrong, and for the other reasons mentioned above. At the same time, God loves divorced people; he is the God of restoration and redemption. He's the God of hope. He is the God who fights for the widow and the orphan; he puts the lonely in families. If you have had the misfortune to suffer divorce know this: God loves you and is for you. He has a future for you, a great future way beyond anything you can imagine. The best years of your life are not in the past; they are yet to come.

Third: sexual intercourse is a spiritual act, not only a physical one. This is why Jesus says that there are grounds for divorce - sexual immorality. The word here is *porneia*, from which we get 'pornography.' It comes from a word meaning *to sell oneself off* and by implication means illicit sexual intercourse. Adam and Eve's marriage comprised covenant vows which were consummated in physical union - they became one flesh. That is important: marriage takes place through covenant vows and subsequent physical union. This is when God accepts that a man and a woman have now become one flesh. Paul takes this up when writing about sexual immorality (1Corinthians 6:12-20). He answers the issue about a man who has sex with a prostitute; he says that the man is now one with her in body and spirit and then quotes Genesis 2:24 - *the two will become one flesh.* Then he uses that to illustrate the believer's relationship to Jesus - *Whoever is united with the Lord is one spirit with him* (verse 17). This statement not only gives us an insight into our oneness with Jesus - we are one spirit with him - it also explains why Jesus in his teaching and the rest of the Word of God allows divorce when illicit sexual intercourse takes place. You become one spirit with that person. Sex is never merely physical; in God's view it is also spiritual. Therefore, if somebody who is married has sex with somebody else, they have broken covenant with their wife or husband and become one spirit with somebody else. Of course, the same principle holds true for single people who have sexual intercourse with somebody: they become one spirit with that person. That is how the Word of God sees it.

Fourth: the collateral damage from unbiblical divorce is enormous: it affects both the offender and the other party. Jesus says that if a man divorces his wife unjustly he makes his wife a victim of adultery; and if people divorce unjustly they become adulterers if they then enter another marriage. I know this raises huge pastoral and ethical issues; hence my desire for sensitivity. I have had to deal with heartbreaking situations many times in pastoral ministry in which people have been divorced for all sorts of reasons. It's far too easy to be harsh and unfeeling and just quote these verses at people; that is why each case must be prayerfully and lovingly considered. Godly wisdom and judgements must be administered. We also have to take into account the teaching of the New Testament epistles, which outwork this in greater detail. We are dispensers of God's hope and justice; of restoration and truth; of love and redemption. I am conscious that this short chapter cannot tackle some of the major questions you might have. Just accept it for what it is: an attempt to explain why Jesus includes marriage and divorce in the Masterplan. It's all a matter of the heart.

Consider/Discuss
What does marriage reveal about the nature of God?

Why does God hate divorce but not divorced people?

EIGHTEEN

YES AND NO

You have heard that it was said to our ancestors, You must not break your oath, but you must keep your oaths to the Lord. But I tell you, don't take an oath at all: either by heaven, because it is God's throne; or by the earth, because it is his footstool; or by Jerusalem, because it is the city of the great King. Neither should you swear by your head, because you cannot make a single hair white or black. But let your word 'yes' be 'yes,' and your 'no' be 'no.' Anything more than this is from the evil one. (Matthew 5:33-37)

We can summarise this part of the Masterplan in one word: integrity. My friend David Lyon defines integrity as the *consistent, complete overlap of our values, words and actions.* Regarding what comes out of our mouths, we speak only the truth, and we don't need to dress it up with anything. As sports-woman Mary Browne said: 'The elegance of honesty needs no adornment.'

'I swear on my mother's grave.' 'I swear on the lives of my children.' 'I swear by all that is holy.' These are modern equivalents of what Jesus is concerned with here. In Jesus' time on earth, oath-taking was common - it was also widely abused. The Old Testament made provision for taking oaths and making vows - covenants were made through them, for example. Moses taught about oaths: *Fear Yahweh your God, worship him and take your oaths in his name* (Deuteronomy 6:13). Such oaths were meant to be signs of allegiance to God: that the oath-taker was a worshipper of God and not a follower of the foreign gods and idols of the nations. Therefore their oaths could be trusted. When Jesus said in Matthew 5:33: *You have heard it was said to our ancestors, You must not break your oath, but you must keep your oaths to the Lord,* he was referring to several Old Testament passages which mention this practice (Leviticus 19:12; Numbers 30:2; Deuteronomy 23:21), all of which were designed to safeguard the sanctity of making oaths to God and taking them in his name. To invoke God in an oath was an immensely important thing to do: it was a matter of life and death. God took such things seriously: to use him to back up the truth of one's words was - and is - no light matter. To make false oaths, to violate or renege on an oath made to God or before God is a grave thing.

In Jesus' time, as I've said, this making of oaths had often degenerated into empty words. As is the case today, words were sometimes cheap. People had even substituted things that represented God - heaven, earth, Jerusalem, one's head - to add to their oaths. They thought: 'If I put God in my oath then people will believe me.' Sadly, when one's words spoken with the added ingredient of God don't add up with corresponding values and actions, not only is the speaker proved to be a liar, God's integrity is also brought into question. We should also note that God swears oaths - he swears by himself:

When God made a promise to Abraham, since He had no one greater to swear by, He swore by Himself: I will indeed bless you, and I will greatly multiply you. (Hebrews 6:13-14)

Because God is faithful, trustworthy, and the God who keeps every promise he makes, he is able to use himself as the standard of integrity and truthfulness. In this example the writer to the Hebrews explains how Abraham could trust God: because God made him a promise. All that God said was, *'I will...'* That was enough for Abraham. God simply said it; he didn't need to dress it up with any additional explanations. He just said it. Sometimes in the Old Testament God emphasises his promise and purpose with a phrase such as, *'As surely as I live,'* which simply means: 'my very existence depends on my integrity.'

Jesus is very direct in his instruction regarding oaths. He says that when it comes to making promises, or even in our everyday conversations, our words must be sufficient in themselves. Don't embellish them with flowery promises or even with invocations of God. In fact, we don't need to back up our promises or conversations with any claims or reference to God at all - we just say 'yes' and 'no.' How can people trust us, that we are telling the truth, that we will keep our word, that we will do what we say? Because our word is enough. When a disciple of Jesus Christ speaks he or she always speaks the truth - we are the pure in heart and every word that comes from our mouth wells up from that pure heart (see Matthew 12:33-

37, where Jesus tells us that at the final judgement we will be justified or condemned by our words, not only by our actions). Nothing else is necessary: our word is sufficient.

Jesus warns us that going beyond the simple yes and no *'comes from the evil one.'* Take special note of that. We know that the devil is a liar and the father of lies (John 8:44). He is an expert in the spoken lie, deception, the broken promise, rumour, gossip and innuendo. He uses these weapons to great effect. His first recorded words in the Word of God cast doubt on the integrity of God by attacking God's words - *'did God really say?'* (Genesis 3:1). That's his ultimate aim - to make God out to be a liar. If he can do that through God's own people who sometimes tragically say one thing and do another, who don't keep their word - their yes and no - who make promises and then break them or fail to fulfil them, then he damages the very integrity of God himself. People often get their concept of God from observing and interacting with his people. If we are those who keep our word and thus maintain our integrity, we display what God is really like. There are high-ranging consequences to our words.

There are many practical implications to all this; and if you are open and honest with him, the Holy Spirit will speak to you regarding how this must be expressed in your life. Let me just say this in conclusion: we as Christians make much of taking God at his word, and rightly so. However, we must also be aware that God takes us at our word too (Deuteronomy 23:21-23). Let your 'yes' be 'yes' be carried through in your actions. Have integrity. Your word is your bond.

Consider/Discuss
What have you promised God? Have you kept that promise?

Have you given your word to anybody and not yet fulfilled that word?

Are you known as somebody whose word is your bond?

NINETEEN

TURN THE OTHER CHEEK

You have heard that it was said, An eye for an eye and a tooth for a tooth. But I tell you, don't resist an evildoer. On the contrary, if anyone slaps you on your right cheek, turn the other to him also. (Matthew 5:38-39)

I'm sure you have heard this phrase 'turn the other cheek' hundreds if not thousands of times. It has taken root in the English language to encourage a certain attitude and way of behaving: that we should be prepared to accept abuse and insult, and not seek revenge or retribution. To turn the other cheek and not to retaliate is regarded as a noble thing - 'just walk away.' For Jesus' disciples, however, it means much more than that.

The principle and practice of eye for eye and tooth for tooth was part of a much larger, comprehensive system of community justice that God instituted for his people in the Old Testament. That is important to establish in our understanding: this was community justice, not individual revenge or retaliation. The practice of eye for eye is mentioned three times (Exodus 21:24; Leviticus 24:20; Deuteronomy 19:21). On each occasion, it occurs in the wider context of how the people of God responded when wrong was done to them, specifically through personal injury caused by fights, acts of violence or accidents. If one's eye was lost, then the maximum penalty that could be inflicted on the perpetrator was the same - their own eye. The punishment fitted the crime. If you took my tooth I could not take your eye; if you broke my arm I could not sever yours. If you wounded me, I could not kill you. Of course, I could choose to forgive you and not require your punishment. And if I did require it, then it would be confirmed first by the community. This was not something that happened in the heat of the moment, when feelings ran high and emotions were raw. Eye for eye was designed to exercise objective, dispassionate community retribution and justice.

It was intended to quench the desire for personal revenge and control the retaliatory excesses of natural people. By the time of Jesus, however, the Pharisees had made it a legalistic practice, like so many other aspects of the Old Testament law. They removed, to all intents and purposes, any spirit of forgiveness. You can see the Pharisees' heart all over the Gospels; it was their intense legalism and externalism that Jesus constantly tackled in his ministry. He does it again here.

Does Jesus mean that we should literally turn our faces to our assailants when they physically attack us, so they can continue their assault? No he doesn't. How do we know that? Because Jesus himself didn't do so when he was hit in the face. If you read John 18:19-23 you will see that when he was on trial Jesus was punched in the face (he was also beaten about the head and body, and spat on). Instead of offering his face again for another blow he spoke to his attackers and challenged them. Likewise, Paul, when he appeared before the Jewish Council, was struck on the mouth under orders from Ananias the high priest. Instead of silently offering his face again for continued violence he spoke out against those who had abused and attacked him. If Jesus means we should literally offer ourselves for further physical attack and abuse when we are hit, then both he and Paul failed. Jesus couldn't even keep his own teaching! Of course, he is the perfect law-keeper and sinless Son of God. If he doesn't mean that his disciples literally offer themselves for continued abuse, what does he mean?

Jesus shows us how to respond to those who do us wrong or who set out to harm us, those who take advantage of us, who presume upon us, who give us no value. He's not talking about our response to physical violence. In this instance, Jesus talks about those who do evil to us - he says don't resist the evildoer. This word 'resist' is a common New Testament word and comes from the word *'to stand.'* It's used when referring to our opposition to the devil in James 4:7 and 1Peter 5:9, where, like its use here, it means *to stand against*. More specifically, the term means *to establish one's own position publicly by conspicuously holding one's ground, refusing to be pushed back, to strongly resist an opponent*. Jesus says that when an evildoer slaps you on the right cheek don't resist him. This is the key: the 'slap on the right cheek.' Jesus' hearers immediately understood his meaning: the slap on the right cheek was done with the back of the right hand. It was regarded as an insult, not a sustained physical assault. It was a back-handed, contemptuous slap across the face, designed to degrade and demean somebody, to get them angry and provoke them, or to mock them. To use our terminology - to wind them up. Jesus says that we have to see it for what it is and not to respond in kind. When this kind of wrong is done to us, don't seek personal revenge, don't retaliate - 'offer the other cheek too.' Don't react to such insults by behaving in the same way; turn the situation on its head. Respond in such a way as to astound the one who is insulting you. In 'offering the other cheek' you're not just walking away, perhaps fuming on the inside! Your attitude is in total contrast to the one who is insulting you; it shows that what they say has no effect on you at all. This is the key: your turning the other cheek is an act of forgiveness. They have done you wrong and you could act in an 'eye to eye' way. But you choose a better path, the path of forgiveness, of overlooking the insult. It has no effect on you: to use a modern idiom, it's like 'water off a duck's back.'

So Jesus encourages us to be pro-active in controlling such situations; he wants us to be self-controlled (better to say, to be under the control of the Holy Spirit), to be bigger than the one who insults us. Don't be so concerned about your own reputation, rights or dignity; leave it to the Lord. The flesh will want to strike out with revenge and retaliation - verbal or physical. Hatred and bitterness can creep in, unless we yield to the Holy Spirit in the situation. Notice that Jesus doesn't take it any further than the left cheek; he doesn't say that if the evildoer slaps that one then offer him the right one again! You're not a punchbag, spiritual or physical.

In a nutshell, Jesus is teaching us not to be concerned about revenge or retaliation when insults come our way, those personal 'slaps on the cheek' that may rile us, hurt us and make us want to get even. I always find this verse helpful at these times:

Beloved, never avenge yourselves, but leave it to the wrath of God, for it is written, "Vengeance is mine, I will repay, says the Lord." (Romans 12:19)

Just leave it to the Lord to sort out - you move on and live in blessing and peace. Your heavenly Father will ensure that you get justice, even if it's not in this life on earth. He is the Judge who always does the right thing at the right time.

In conclusion, I need to say something to those who suffer physical violence from family members, and to any who are victims of domestic abuse in all its forms - mental, physical, sexual. You might be reading this and are in the tragic position of being such a victim. Please don't think that Jesus wants you to suffer in silence and remain where you are; this passage of Scripture cannot be used by others to justify imprisoning you in your situation. Jesus does not intend for you to live in such circumstances where abuse and violence are perpetrated against you; you are called to live in safety and peace, not in pain, fear and dread. If you are in such a situation, please seek help, wherever you can get it. God loves you and cares for you and will make a way out for you.

Consider/Discuss
What 'winds you up?'

What practical ways do you 'turn the other cheek?'

TWENTY

THE EXTRA MILE

If someone wants to sue you and take your tunic, let him have your cloak as well. If someone forces you to go one mile, go with him two miles. Give to the one who asks you, and do not turn away from the one who wants to borrow from you. (Matthew 5:40-42)

Have you noticed how many of Jesus' sayings in the Masterplan have become woven into our everyday language? They are used by all kinds of people - politicians, educators, sociologists, non-Christian religious teachers, even atheists - as examples of a moral code or pattern of life that anybody may aspire to, whether they are Christians or not. They have become a humanitarian manifesto. However, Jesus never intended his teaching to be applied like that - he was addressing his disciples. I say that because we are discovering that Jesus' expectations of us are incredible: our lives are to be radically different from the rest of society. We meet that again here. Jesus has just taught us how to respond to insults and abuse ('turn the other cheek'); now he complements that with the other side of the coin: the issue of self-assertion - the insistence on getting our own way.

In Jesus' time Jewish men wore two garments - an inner one, usually of basic quality, and a better quality outer one. Jesus says that if someone sues you to take away your inner garment, give him the outer one too. The word 'sue' occurs twice more in the New Testament - in Acts 25:9 and Revelation 11:18 - where it is used to describe *somebody standing trial or being judged*. It's legal terminology. The word 'take' means an *aggressive assertiveness, to take hold of something forcefully or violently*. The Law of Moses was categorical regarding taking someone's clothes from them - *If you ever take your neighbour's cloak as collateral, return it to him before sunset* (Exodus 22:26). In legal disputes your adversary could take your cloak as collateral while you found the money to pay him your debt, or while the courts deliberated on the case. But he had to return it every night so you would not be exposed to the elements. This was a legal right for all. Nobody was to go to bed cold; that was your right in the Law.

Jesus takes this example from life and uses hyperbole again to make his point: don't be constantly concerned about your rights. Don't keep resisting people and insisting on fighting for things that you think should be justifiably yours all the time. Don't be consumed with getting what is rightfully yours - be the opposite and give yourself away (give the outer, more expensive cloak as well as the inner one). Please don't think that Jesus is telling us to give all our clothes away and walk around naked! He is not being literal here; he is not giving us a prescribed list of what to do in specific instances. He is teaching us guiding principles, leaving us to apply them as different circumstances occur.

Let me say something very important at this point. Jesus is not saying that Christians should never stand up for their legal rights. If he did, then the apostle Paul utterly failed in that regard. When he and Silas were arrested in Philippi (Acts 16) he was asked by the authorities to leave the city quietly and not cause a fuss. He refused and demanded that the magistrates themselves escort them publicly from the city. Today, in the United Kingdom, Christians have to go to court and to tribunals because they are being sued or have lost their jobs: a registrar who refuses to conduct 'same sex marriages'; a baker who refuses to accept an order for an event celebrating homosexuality; an airline worker banned from wearing a cross on her necklace. Are these Christians wrong because they pursue a legal process? Should they just be quiet, 'give the outer garment' and go home? Not at all. Jesus just means here that in our everyday, personal life, his disciples are not concerned about asserting ourselves, trying to get our own way all the time. That is all. Like every other citizen Christians have their rights in law; and where they believe the law is unjust or anti-Christian they not only have the right but the duty to stand up and be counted.

Go the extra mile: we probably hear this phrase more than any of the other sayings of Jesus from the Masterplan. In Jesus' time the Roman occupiers could force anybody to carry a load for one mile. That is how they often transported material around the empire; it was a form of free labour and meant they didn't have to carry things themselves. Obviously it was open to abuse; the local populace could be forced to carry anything that the Romans ordered them to for one mile. You can imagine the reactions this would cause. Once the mile was completed the load would be put down and off you went. You'd been inconvenienced, you were hot and sweaty, there would be no reward or word of thanks. You might even have to retrace your steps back the mile you had just walked! It could happen frequently; there was no rota. The person who'd walked the mile was not always in the best frame of mind. Jesus knew that; even though we have no record of it happening to him in the Gospels, it's probable he personally experienced it. Imagine the response and reaction when Jesus says: 'If you're forced to go one mile - go an extra one! Do you see the dramatic effect this will have, not only on your neighbours but on the soldier who compelled you?' This way of life that Jesus advocates was revolutionary: nobody behaved like that. Everybody did only what was required of them, just the bare minimum, and not a step more. Jesus says that his disciples are not like that: our lives are not minimalist, they are maximalist! The Word of God speaks much about the person who is generous - in spirit and time, in money and hospitality, in words and actions (see Proverbs 11:25; 2Corinthians 8:2). It also speaks about the mean person, the stingy person, the one who does only what is required of them and no more. Jesus says his disciples are 'extra mile' people - our generosity and serving is radical and contrary to everything else around us. Paul put it like this:

And whatever you do, in word or in deed, do everything in the name of the Lord Jesus, giving thanks to God the Father through Him. (Colossians 3:17)

Jesus summarises: *'Give to the one who asks you, and don't turn away from the one wants to borrow from you.'* Be open to others; don't be consumed with your own needs and rights. Look out for others; be approachable. Whenever you are able, be the one who meets the needs of others. Be generous. Just a word of caution too: be wise in all your dealings with people. Be led by the Holy Spirit - he will show you exactly what to do in every situation. Be governed by the Word of God; read the Proverbs, they will help you live wisely in this regard. This will also help you understand people's motives and you will learn to avoid those who only want to take advantage of you or exploit you. So be wise and shrewd. Don't be unwise; some people will only want to use you for their own ends and take from you. Be wise in all your dealings; but keep an open heart and a redemptive attitude at all times.

Consider/Discuss
How do you live the 'extra mile' life?

How do you discern between people who need the 'extra mile' and those who just want to take advantage of you?

TWENTY ONE

THE POWER OF LOVE

You have heard that it was said, Love your neighbour and hate your enemy. But I tell you, love your enemies and pray for those who persecute you, so that you may be sons of your Father in heaven. For he causes his sun to rise on the evil and the good, and sends rain on the righteous and the unrighteous. For if you love those who love you, what reward will you have? Don't even the tax collectors do the same? And if you greet only your brothers, what are you doing out of the ordinary? Don't even the Gentiles do the same? Be perfect, therefore, as your heavenly Father is perfect. (Matthew 5:43-48)

It's evident by now that Jesus has an extremely high expectation of his disciples. Thankfully, he has also given us the Holy Spirit, who enables us to live the Masterplan. If we don't realise that then what Jesus says next might well lead us into frustration or make us throw our hands up in exasperation and resignation: love your enemies!

Jesus now refers to the second part of what he calls the Greatest Commandment (see Mark 12:29-31): love your neighbour as yourself. He tells his disciples that until now they have been taught to do that, but at the same time they've been taught that it's acceptable to hate their enemies. But where in the Old Testament does it say such a thing? It doesn't. Jesus is directly contradicting the prevailing teaching of the scribes and the Pharisees, who taught the people to love their neighbour and to hate their enemy (the 'tax collectors' and the 'Gentiles'). This contradicted the Old Testament. Jesus brings us back to live according to the Word of God, and not to follow the religious or philosophical traditions of people. This in itself is a very important principle to live by; the Word of God has to be the controlling and determining factor in everything for us.

Jesus tells us how to respond to those who make themselves, or call themselves, our enemies, who actively oppose us and persecute us (remember how he taught us that persecution is inevitable, in

Matthew 5:10). The standard of the kingdom of God is that we love our enemies and we pray for those who persecute us. Then he gives us the reason why - that we may be sons of our heavenly Father (verse 44). Loving our enemies does something beneficial to us: it helps us mature in our sonship. Christians are children of God (John 1:12). The image of our being children of God explains our new birth: that we have been born again and, just as natural children have a childlike faith, so we have put our faith in God. We belong to the family of God the Father; and our childlike faith in God continues all our lives. However, to be childlike in our faith in no way means that we continue to behave in a childish manner.

That is why the New Testament says that we are not only children of God, we are also sons of God. (Sonship is nothing to do with gender, ladies are sons of God too: Galatians 3:26-29 explains that). Romans 8:15 says we have received the Spirit of sonship or adoption (*huiothesia*, which literally means *the placing of a son*). The Greek word *huios* describes an adult, mature son, as opposed to a baby or child. *Huiothesia* was a technical term used outside the New Testament in which a slave would be adopted by his master into the family and so be put in every respect in exactly the same position and nature as any of the man's natural sons. He became a birth son and possessed the same name, rights, identity, standing, citizenship and inheritance as any of the man's natural sons. He became a true son of his adoptive father. He also had the same responsibilities and obligations as his brothers. He had a new identity and all the privileges and responsibilities which accompanied that new identity. Sonship goes to the core of our identity as disciples: we are meant to mature, to grow up to our full potential as children of God.

Loving our enemies is a family trait; it's a hallmark of being a mature son of God. Our heavenly Father is also like that - he loved the world so much that he gave his Only Son (John 3:16) - yet the world hated him; it still does. When you love your enemy he is no longer your enemy. Something happens inside you as a son of God which causes you to see him as your Father sees him, and your attitude towards him changes. He might well still see himself as your enemy and wish to remain your enemy: but that is his issue, not yours. You might not sit down together and share a meal; he might not want to talk to you. He may well continue to act badly towards you and say all kinds of terrible things about you. He might still want to harm you, or worse. But you now see him differently. You love him. The word Jesus uses here for love is *agapē* - the God kind of love. Only God can love like this - and those who are his sons. That's why the life Jesus describes in the Masterplan is a life lived under the Lordship of Jesus and the control of the Holy Spirit.

Jesus tells us to love not only those people we find easy to love, or to merely love our own - anybody can do that. There's nothing remarkable in loving people who are lovable or who love us. Jesus' disciples are radically different. We live a life out of the ordinary; our lives shock others because they manifest Jesus. What sets us apart from the world is that we are able to cross the divide of enmity and love those who hate us and call themselves our enemies. God's love is an active love; it's not just having the feelings of love. It's a fixed attitude which doesn't depend on whether the object of our love reciprocates. That's why Paul highlighted its incredible power in that wonderful chapter on love - 1Corinthians 13.

Jesus sets the bar very high for us: *'be perfect as your heavenly Father is perfect'*. That word 'perfect' means *complete, or whole*, and is used many times in the New Testament to describe the maturity of believers. Basically, Jesus tells us to stop being childish and to grow up, and to represent our heavenly Father here on earth as his sons. How? By behaving as God does, and to love those who hate us. Even though the bar is high it's what Jesus expects; he loved his enemies. If he could do it so can we.

Consider/Discuss
Are there people who call themselves your enemy?

If so, how do you express God's love to them?

TWENTY TWO

SECRET GIVERS

Be careful not to practise your righteousness in front of people, to be seen by them. Otherwise, you will have no reward from your Father in heaven. So whenever you give to the poor, don't sound a trumpet before you, as the hypocrites do in the synagogues and on the streets to be applauded by people. I assure you: They've got their reward! But when you give to the poor, don't let your left hand know what your right hand is doing, so that your giving may be in secret. And your Father who sees in secret will reward you. (Matthew 6:1-4)

When I was involved in pastoral ministry, one of my more pleasant tasks was to act as a vehicle of blessing. Sometimes, members of the church would come to me with an envelope containing money. They would ask me to pass it on to another brother or sister in the fellowship whom they wanted to bless anonymously. They were aware that this person was in need and wanted to help them. I would go to the person in question with the envelope and say, 'I've been asked to give you this.' If they wanted to know who it was from, I'd say, 'It's from the Lord.' They understood that one of their brothers or sisters wanted to bless them without drawing attention to themselves. They were always overwhelmed by the kindness of their friends and would most often say something like, 'Please thank the Lord for me!'

This wasn't the only way the Body of Christ met each other's needs; sometimes they would do so directly. The main thing was that in all my experience nobody ever made a song and dance about what Jesus called 'practising our righteousness'. My fellow believers lived by this principle that Jesus lays out for us in the Masterplan.

Jesus contrasts two ways of living: the ostentatious, religious hypocrite, and the unassuming disciple. We will discover over the course of future chapters that Jesus deals with three specific areas where hypocritical self-righteousness can rear its ugly head: prayer, fasting, and, here, in our giving. We constantly see that the life of the disciple is totally contrary to that of the natural world and to religion, both of which exalt themselves over God and others. Here Jesus warns us not to draw attention to ourselves in the way we give; to use a modern idiom: don't blow your own trumpet!

Jesus often spoke about money; the Gospels are full of references to it. One of the most misquoted verses in the entire New Testament is about money: *The love of money is a root of all kinds of evil* (1Timothy 6:10). Money is not the root of all evil: the *love* of money is a root of all kinds of evil. If you want to know somebody's heart, see how they handle money. Jesus teaches us how to use our money in the way we give to others; he uses the example of the poor, though the principle remains across the board regarding the way we give. Jesus makes certain assumptions about his disciples, one of which is that we are givers. By our very nature we are generous people and are quick to meet the needs of others. That is a fundamental characteristic of Christians: we are not mean and stingy, but kind and generous. There is a saying about mean people: they have short arms and deep pockets! Christians are not like that. Whenever we meet the needs of others - not only the poor - we should do so in a certain way; Jesus calls it giving in secret. Don't draw attention to yourself, don't make grand gestures or big announcements about it: just do it quietly. The way my brothers and sisters used me to be their messenger is a great example of secret giving.

At the core is our motives for our actions: why do we act in the way we do? Jesus calls those who trumpet their giving as hypocrites; the word comes from the world of the theatre and describes an actor - somebody playing a part, pretending to be what they're not. That is what's going on with those who make a big fuss about themselves and their righteous acts - they're play-acting. That's what self-righteousness does: it pretends to be real righteousness but it's phoney. Self-righteous people are fakes; they act in such a way as to convey something they're not.

These hypocrites also think that their money gains them control or influence over others. Not only does it make them look good, they think the way they use it in the church buys them status and privileges. I have met leaders who've been controlled by people in their churches, who regard themselves as the major financial contributors in the church. They use that supposed power and influence to try and lever the leaders into doing what they want. It's a form of bribery. When the leader resists them they threaten to leave and take their money, their influence, with them. The wise leader will show them the door, what a friend of mine calls 'the right foot of fellowship!' Never use your giving to assert your will or personal agenda on to God's kingdom - that's what Ananias and Sapphira tried to do, with catastrophic results (see Acts 5:1-11). They paid with their lives.

We must not overlook what Jesus says about God the Father here - he is a rewarder. There is an interesting verse in Proverbs: *Whoever is kind to the poor lends to Yahweh, and he will reward them for what they have done* (Proverbs 19:17). It's true that God owns everything and has no lack or need (Psalm 50:10). Yet when the righteous are kind to the poor - including meeting financial needs and alleviating poverty - God takes notice and he rewards the giver. In doing this we lend to the Lord - and he not only repays us, he rewards us. This is an aspect of the law of sowing and reaping. You don't give just to receive; neither do you give and not expect to receive. Reaping is an inevitable consequence of sowing. When you sow expect to reap, so you can sow more. If you're a secret, generous giver, get ready for God to reward you, so that you can be blessed and continue to be a blessing, in increasing measures.

Consider/Discuss
How do you meet the needs of others?

How does God reward you for your generosity to others?

When you sow do you expect to reap?

TWENTY THREE

THE SECRET PLACE

Whenever you pray, you must not be like the hypocrites, because they love to pray standing in the synagogues and on the street corners to be seen by people. I assure you: They've got their reward! But when you pray, go into your secret place, shut your door, and pray to your Father who is in secret. And your Father, who sees in secret, will reward you. When you pray, don't babble like the idolaters, since they imagine they'll be heard for their many words. Don't be like them, because your Father knows the things you need before you ask him. (Matthew 6:5-8)

We are in the middle of a section of the Masterplan, in which Jesus contrasts the life of the hypocrite and the disciple. In the previous chapter, we saw that Jesus warns us against behaving like the former: those who love to show off their self-righteousness with great public gestures, drawing attention to themselves and away from God. He tells us that the way of his disciples is quite different; he uses the word 'secret' several times here to explain what he means. The word is *kryptō*, which means *hidden* or *inward*, as well as *secret*. Jesus says that a hallmark of his disciples is that they pray; they often spend time with their heavenly Father in what Jesus describes as 'the secret place.' It is a picture of the intimate fellowship that we enjoy with God: times when it's just him and us, when we can pray to him, listen to him, and be transformed by him. Prayer in the secret place is never wasted time; it puts all other time into perspective. There is an old adage: if you're too busy to pray, then you're too busy. Is Jesus talking about a real place where we need to go to pray in private to God? Yes, he is; it's something that should be an essential aspect of our relationship with our heavenly Father.

However, Jesus isn't confining prayer exclusively to a specific time and place; it's not a religious activity to be exercised in the way the hypocrites did it. Rather, he highlights something of the true nature of prayer, homing in on the importance of being alone with God, to be able to converse with him without outward show or distraction. Prayer can be done 'on the wing' so to speak, in any moment, anywhere and any time. It is done in the gathering of the church, with a friend over coffee or while sharing the Word of God together. Prayer can be made in the heat of battle or on the operating table, quietly while in class or at the top of one's voice while walking in the mountains. Prayer can be exultant or intense, rejoicing and thankful, heart-rending and tearful, in times of joy and grief. Prayer is for every occasion. Prayer can be one word or many. Prayer is a two-way conversation with our heavenly Father, in which we listen to him and speak to him. My Bible College Principal called prayer 'the Christian's vital breath.' Our 'breathing in' in prayer is the time we spend listening to our Father. Jesus emphasises this when he says we are not to babble with many words, thinking that God will respond simply because of the amount of things we say. Prayer in the secret place is primarily listening to the voice of God. Then we 'breathe out' in response to what we have heard our Father say. Thus we pray according to his word and his will. Genuine prayer always originates in heaven; that is its power.

All other kinds of prayer are effective only if we have our 'secret place' prayer life in order. That's why Jesus emphasises it as a necessity for every disciple: regular time spent alone with God, in the secret place. He speaks of somewhere you can go where there are no other distractions. You know where God wants to meet you. When you get there, 'shut the door' - block out all other things. Turn off the computer, the phone, the television. Avoid crowds and the distractions of social media. Let it just be you and the God of the secret place, who is waiting for you to seek him so you can find him and he can reveal himself to you.

That's the true beauty of prayer in secret. God is in the secret place. Yes, he is omnipresent, he is everywhere; but Jesus says he can be uniquely met in the secret place. The Word of God speaks about seeking God and finding him:

You will call to me and come and pray to me. You will seek me and find me when you search for me with all your heart. (Jeremiah 29:12-13)

Jesus gives two further insights into the character of the God who is in the secret place. *Firstly,* in verse 6, he says that the Father will reward us when we spend time with him there. He isn't paying us for the privilege of being with us; we are not hiring ourselves out to God to keep him company and being paid by him for our effort. Our motive for being in the secret place is not to get anything; our sole motive is to be with our Father in a unique way. But such is the nature of God that he makes our time with him worthwhile; he 'rewards' us. The benefits of spending time with God one-on-one are enormous. *Secondly,* Jesus says in verse 8 that even before we get into the secret place, our heavenly Father knows what we need. God knows everything about everything and everything about everybody. Nothing takes him by surprise; you can never tell him something he doesn't already know. God is not an adviser, who listens to you and then works out what to do. He is the answer to all your questions. You just need to spend time with him, so that he can tell you what you need to hear.

How do we pray when we enter the secret place? When we have listened it's time to pray, to 'breathe out.' Thankfully, Jesus tells us how to pray: we call it the Lord's Prayer, and we will begin to unpack that next.

Consider/Discuss
Where is your secret place?

How do you ensure you spend regular time there with your heavenly Father?

How do you recognise God's voice?

TWENTY FOUR

OUR FATHER IN HEAVEN

> *You should pray like this: Our Father in heaven, Your name be honoured as holy. (Matthew 6:9)*

We come now to some of the most famous sentences in the English language, let alone in the Word of God. We call them The Lord's Prayer. We have discovered that Jesus speaks of the secret place where we meet God in prayer. Having established the need for such a place Jesus turns his attention to how we pray: *'You should pray like this.'*

One of the great tragedies of religion is that it has reduced what Jesus gave us as a structure for meaningful prayer to a liturgical exercise in which the words are recited by rote. Jesus never intended his teaching on prayer to be merely repeating his words verbatim: he is laying out for us a structure, a form, in which he gives us the necessary ingredients for our times of prayer in the secret place. I'm not saying that everyone who has ever recited the words of the Lord's Prayer has wasted their time. I myself have prayed it sincerely like that thousands of times in my life, and did it just the other day at a funeral. I'm merely saying that it's more than that; it's meant to be the basis of how we pray and what we pray when we are alone with God.

As we have been reminded several times in the Masterplan, Jesus is concerned with the state of our hearts. He demonstrates that again in his instructions on prayer. When we come before God to pray we first of all come in an attitude of worship. This is how Jesus expresses it:

> *Our Father in heaven, your name be honoured as holy. (Matthew 6:9)*

Worship is the gateway to prayer; we don't come before God just to present to him our needs, concerns, and requests. All those have their rightful place, but not the first place. When we pray, we begin with who God is - we worship and praise him, we acknowledge that we are in the presence of the one, true, living God, the Creator of the universe. Our attitude and language, therefore, is worshipful, reverential, honouring and truthful. This is a wonderful first sentence by Jesus, packed full of revelation, yet simple in its explanation of how we approach God in prayer. Notice the first word: *Our*. Right at the beginning of our prayer we are reminded that we are part of a great worldwide family of believers. Even though we may be alone in our room with God, at the same time we are part of a vast kingdom family - the church. This is demonstrated by the second word and the completion of the phrase: 'our *Father* in heaven.' Our status in Christ before God is one of sonship (Galatians 3:26-29); he is our Father. The biblical image of God as a Father is not a human one: God is not like a human father only infinitely better. He is a different kind of Father altogether. He is God the Father; he is not, as seems to be the fashion today, my 'daddy' God. While it may satisfy some kind of need in us, it's rather an inadequate way of looking at God as our Father.

Our Father is in heaven; what a fantastic way to come to him! God rules and reigns over all things from heaven. He sees all things from heaven; the heavenly hosts are at his command; all the resources of heaven are available to us when we pray. Because we are in the heavenly realms in Christ (Ephesians 1:3), we also pray from a heavenly perspective, even though we are in our secret place on earth. When we pray, heaven invades earth. So, when you pray, come before the Lord and spend time worshipping him before you ask anything of him. Praise your heavenly Father, come before him the way he has prescribed: with thanksgiving and praise (Psalm 100:4). Tell him how great he is, not to soften him up for your requests, but because he is the mighty God who is to be glorified. He is worthy of all your praise and adoration.

The final instruction Jesus gives us as we come to our heavenly Father is for us to be acutely aware just who we are coming to: the One whose name is to be honoured as holy (older translations have *hallowed*). This term means *'to revere, venerate, respect, honour as holy'*. Note that Jesus mentions God's holiness here; out of all of God's attributes he highlights this particular one. Not God's love or grace, not God's mercy or kindness, not God's faithfulness or power. He speaks about God's holiness. Of course, no attribute of God functions in isolation from the others, and no attribute of God has priority over the others. God is the sum of all his attributes, and he works in the totality of all his attributes all the time. However, we cannot escape the fact that Jesus tells us to come before God in prayer with an awareness and deep appreciation of his holiness. God's holiness reveals to us how pure and clean he is in his nature and character. The fact is that we are unable to appreciate how holy God is. We might try to imagine something pure and clean and multiply that sense of purity even by a trillion: we wouldn't come anywhere close to the holiness of God. We know nothing like God's holiness; we cannot compare it to anything. Since God is infinite (unlimited), he is infinitely holy. God's holiness is unique, incomprehensible, unapproachable and unattainable (1Samuel 2:2; Exodus 15:11). The miracle of salvation in which God takes unrighteous sinners and makes us saints - holy ones - is amazing! We who were once unholy are now able, because of the perfect sacrifice of Jesus the Holy One, to enter the secret place in the fear of God but without fear of destruction or rejection. We come in faith by the power of the Holy Spirit to worship and fellowship our heavenly, holy Father. Never take God for granted or become over-familiar with him. Yes he is your Father; he's also a consuming fire of holiness. He welcomes you into his presence in love and grace, and he enjoys being with you. Nevertheless, he is unimaginably holy: he isn't your 'buddy' or your 'daddy' or 'the man upstairs.' He is God.

Consider/Discuss
How much of your prayer in the secret place is spent praising and worshipping God?

What does it mean for you to know that your Father in heaven is holy?

TWENTY FIVE

PRAYING THE KINGDOM

Your kingdom come. Your will be done on earth as it is in heaven. (Matthew 6:10)

Having established the attitude with which we come to our heavenly Father in the secret place of prayer, Jesus lays out the first thing we concern ourselves with in prayer: the kingdom of God. Prayer is not primarily about us and our needs, even though, as we will discover, that is a valid and necessary aspect of prayer. In effect Jesus says to us, 'Make the kingdom of God your priority' (which he actually says in chapter 6:33). Here he explains what he means: *'Father, your will be done on earth as it is in heaven.'* In a nutshell: the kingdom of God is all to do with the will of God. God's will is exercised without question or opposition in heaven. Jesus instructs us to pray that it will also be done on earth in precisely the same way. Therefore, we can say that the kingdom of God is where the will of God is done - without question or opposition. Of course, 'earth' begins with me: I can't pray that the will of God be done everywhere without it first of all being done - without question or opposition - in me. God's kingdom is God's will.

I want to take this opportunity to explain some more things about the kingdom of God. The kingdom of God is mentioned directly almost 300 times in the Word of God, and is a major theme of both the Old and New Testaments. The kingdom of God is the right of God to rule as God; it's God's authority, reign, power and government. It's his kingly rule; God exercises his authority through his kingdom. The kingdom of God is the realm in which God rules. Wherever you see words or phrases in the Word of God about rule, reign, thrones, governments, they are all kingdom words. The Word of God is clear - Yahweh reigns over everything and everybody (Psalm 97:1).

Every kingdom is an expression of its king; the kingdom of God is no exception. It expresses the life and nature of God; it manifests the will of God. The church is the kingdom community; disciples are citizens of the kingdom of God. Always remember the kingdom of God, while it includes the church, is greater than the church. The church exists to manifest the kingdom; the kingdom expresses itself through the church. If you like, the church is the vehicle of the kingdom. Jesus mentioned the church only twice but he taught about the kingdom of God many times (the parables, for example, are mostly about the kingdom). The church is vital in God's purpose: it represents his kingdom on earth. Jesus is the King of the kingdom of God; and 'Jesus is Lord' is the cry of his kingdom people. The church has meaning and relevance to God and the world only to the extent that it represents the kingdom of God and its King - the Lord Jesus.

When we receive Jesus as Lord we enter the kingdom of God (John 3:3; Romans 14:17). In that sense the kingdom of God has truly come into us through the Holy Spirit. What does Jesus mean, then, when he tells us to pray, 'Your kingdom come?' Let me highlight three aspects of the kingdom that will help us in our prayers concerning it.

First: the kingdom of God lasts forever (Psalm 145:13; Luke 1:33). Unlike every other kingdom, empire or world power, the kingdom of God will never crumble, decline or pass away. It's an everlasting kingdom because it's the kingdom of the everlasting God. The kingdom of God is here to stay. All human institutions are temporary, even if they last hundreds of years; but the kingdom of God is permanent. We pray with absolute confidence to a God who cannot be shaken, whose rule and reign are established. We come to Jesus, whose kingly throne is secure. The ground of our faith is in the God who rules over all things. To pray, 'Your kingdom come' is a declaration of who God is and of who we are in Christ. He is the King of the everlasting kingdom; the foundation on which we pray is therefore secure.

Second: the kingdom of God increases and grows forever. Isaiah 9:7 says: *Of the increase of his government and peace there will be no end.* The kingdom of God not only lasts forever, it also increases forever. It doesn't just last in perpetuity, going on and on, but staying the same. That would be good, but the kingdom of God is more than that: it's a kingdom that lasts in increasing measures and increasing dimensions forever. The kingdom of God is an infinite, unlimited kingdom, because it's the kingdom of the infinite, unlimited God. The kingdom of God doesn't just spread everywhere: it also expands in all aspects everywhere, throughout the entire universe. This ever-increasing kingdom is now in us through the Holy Spirit. When we pray 'Your kingdom come,' we are expressing to our heavenly Father that we want the kingdom of God to increase and grow within us. That's why the New Testament teaches that while we are completely righteous in Christ, we still grow in measures of faith and in maturity of character. Our prayer in the secret place regarding the kingdom allows the Holy Spirit to continue to increase the kingdom in us. We also pray with a sense of correct perspective on everything else: if we understand that the kingdom is increasing then the manner of our praying will be in accord with that understanding. We pray bigger prayers: we understand that the kingdom of God is at work throughout the world. Every time somebody is born again the kingdom advances. Every miracle, healing, sign and wonder advances the kingdom. Every maturing Christian is evidence of the increasing kingdom. When we pray with a kingdom mindset we view everything with kingdom eyes.

Third: we are always receiving the kingdom. Hebrews 12:28 says: *since we are receiving a kingdom that cannot be shaken, let us be thankful.* While it's true that the kingdom of God is in us, we are also continuously receiving it. Don't be confused by that; it's a common New Testament principle. The kingdom has come, the kingdom is coming, the kingdom will come. We always live with a sense of now and not yet; we have it and there is more to receive of it. This phrase *we are receiving a kingdom* indicates an ongoing, active reception on our part. The New Testament word *receive* means *to take by showing strong personal initiative, to take aggressively, to take to oneself.* It's the opposite of passivity. To receive the kingdom means we actively and continuously embrace the kingdom with all that we are. It's a constant mindset in which we always embrace the ever increasing kingdom as God stretches us in our faith and in our capacity. That means we always live in the now of God; we don't live in the nostalgic past or defer to the future what the Lord wants to achieve in us now. In continuously receiving the kingdom of God we are always moving forward in God's kingdom purpose. Therefore, our times of prayer in the secret place are encounters with the God of an everlasting, increasing kingdom, and we pray accordingly. Every time we pray, 'Your kingdom come', we change.

Consider/Discuss

How does praying the kingdom affect your perspective of the world?

What evidence do you see of the kingdom increasing in the world and in your life?

TWENTY SIX

NECESSARY BREAD

Give us today our daily bread. (Matthew 6:11)

Our Father in heaven is the God of today, the God of the immediate. All that he is, he is now. As God Almighty he has all the resources within himself to meet all the needs of all his people at every moment. This is the aspect of God's nature that Jesus now unwraps for us.

Jesus instructs us to pray specifically: 'Father, for the coming day, give us all that is necessary for us to live through this day.' That word 'daily' occurs only here in the New Testament and is used rarely outside of it. It means *what is necessary or sufficient for the moment*, hence what is needed each day. We could translate the phrase as *necessary bread*. Jesus tells us to come to our Father each day and ask him to provide for us all our 'necessary bread' for that day. In many cultures bread is one of the staples of life. It takes many forms, but for billions of people bread is a daily, necessary food. Jesus says that we can trust God for our food each day; our heavenly Father will provide for us. One of my family's favourite verses is this:

I have been young and now I am old; but I have never seen the righteous forsaken or their children begging bread. (Psalm 37:25)

God promises to feed and clothe us: each day we come to him and pray according to that promise. However, Jesus also means more than just asking God to provide physical bread or our necessary food. 'Bread' indicates all that we need to live, everything that is necessary for us to extend the kingdom. Whatever the day brings we can depend on the Lord to give us everything we need to live as overcomers throughout the day. One day we might need peace; he gives it. The next day courage or physical strength; or wisdom, patience, faith. In all probability we will need to exercise the gifts of the Holy Spirit. We will need much 'bread' every day. All the resources of God are constantly available to us to provide those daily needs. All we have to do is ask our heavenly Father for them and receive them from him.

This kind of prayer focuses us on what is truly necessary. It therefore excludes selfishness and self-centredness. When we pray as Jesus instructs us we are no longer self-obsessed or absorbed by our own needs. Jesus said we should pray, 'Give *us*...' - we don't only pray about our own individual needs, we also pray for the various needs and situations of our families and friends, for whoever the Holy Spirit brings to mind. These are not 'shopping list' prayers; we capture our Father's heart for people and pray for them as he leads us. When we pray 'give us' we become more aware of the corporate nature of being a Christian: we are part of a world-wide family. I find that when I pray like this I spend more time praying for the needs of others than my own. I also become more aware that others are praying for me too.

If our focus is on the Lord and we trust him to meet our needs we avoid two pitfalls: first - chasing after wealth and materialism; second - embracing a poverty mentality and unbiblical self-denial. Both these attitudes are dangerous. Proverbs puts it like this:

> *Give me neither poverty nor wealth; feed me with the food I need. Otherwise, I might have too much and deny You, saying, 'Who is Yahweh?' or I might have nothing and steal, profaning the name of my God. (Proverbs 30:8-9)*

I remember a preacher once saying, 'God meets our needs not our greeds.' That preacher was right. If our energy is poured into accumulating things or attaining status and position for ourselves, then we are going to end up frustrated and never fulfilled, because we will always chase after more. In our chapter on the poor in spirit we learned that God isn't against money; he gives us the ability to create wealth (Deuteronomy 8:18). But he doesn't want you to wear yourself out trying to get rich or expend all your energy on accumulating wealth (Proverbs 23:4). If God blesses you with wealth, enjoy it and use it. If you earn a large salary and drive a nice car and live in a big house: no problem at all. Just don't make those things the focus of your life.

An equal danger is a false spirituality that parades itself in the virtue of poverty. Let me repeat something I said earlier: the Bible does not teach that there is any spiritual benefit or value in poverty. Poverty and wealth do not bring a person closer to God. The Word of God never advocates the pursuit of poverty as a spiritual or blessed activity. I have met many genuinely poor people and have been to places in this world where extreme poverty is rife. When I have been in a position to help alleviate poverty I have never had my offer to help refused on the grounds that it would affect that person's spirituality. Too many Christians close themselves off to the material blessings of God because they think that wealth is unspiritual or that being poor equates to humility. God blesses us because he wants to bless us and equally to make us a blessing to others. That's the kind of God he is.

I am discovering that I can pray to my heavenly Father about any need; whatever I or my fellow believers need I can ask God to provide it. I am learning never to say: 'God isn't interested in that; I won't bother him with that.' He's my heavenly Father; I can talk to him about anything and everything.

Ultimately of course our lives don't consist of what we have or don't have (Luke 12:15). In the Old Testament, God declared that we don't live by bread alone but by every word that comes out of his mouth (Deuteronomy 8:3). Jesus quoted this verse to Satan when the latter tempted him to live otherwise (Matthew 4:4). If we live each day by every word that God speaks then we can come each day with a correct perspective on that day and pray accordingly: 'Father, give every one of us all that is necessary for today to live in your kingdom.'

Consider/Discuss
What is your 'necessary bread?'

What is the 'necessary bread' of those you pray for?

TWENTY SEVEN

THE POWER OF FORGIVENESS

Forgive us our debts, as we have also forgiven our debtors. (Matthew 6:12)

For if you forgive people their wrongdoing, your heavenly Father will forgive you as well. But if you don't forgive people, your Father will not forgive your wrongdoing. (Matthew 6:14-15)

We have discovered that Christian discipleship is inherently corporate. Jesus didn't call only one disciple to follow him: he initially called twelve, who for three years lived together, worked together, learned together, and overcame together. They came to depend on one another and eventually to love and appreciate each other. Along the way they offended each other, bumped heads and clashed, even debating which of them was the greatest! One of them even betrayed Jesus and his friends. Yet Jesus was able to leave a committed community of 120 men and women who together experienced the power of Pentecost; they were added to by another 3,000 on that historic day. All the images of the Church in the New Testament are corporate; Christianity knows nothing of the individualistic, unaccountable, independent disciple. We have already learned that God is *our* Father; we pray 'Give *us…our* daily bread.' Jesus now addresses a fundamental aspect of our corporate life: how we react and respond if we sin against each other.

There are several words in the New Testament which describe sin. The words Jesus uses in verses 12 and 14 are different: in verse 12 the word means *a debt, something that is owed, an offence, a fault committed against somebody*. It's sometimes used to describe something we should have done but failed to do, hence we are indebted to somebody. In verse 14 the word means *a false step, a lapse, a wrongdoing, to deviate from the truth, to transgress.* Older versions of the Word of God translate both these verses with the word 'trespass'.

When we enter the secret place it's vital that there are no hindrances to our prayers, that there no barriers between us and God, or between us and our fellow disciples. So Jesus tells us to ask God for forgiveness if we need to; note that - *if* we need to. If there is nothing between you and God and between you and another, then don't go looking for something that is not there. If there is anything amiss the Holy Spirit will soon let you know. In verse 14 Jesus reveals something about the nature of God's forgiveness: in certain circumstances it's conditional. If we refuse to forgive others then he won't forgive us. We can't expect to ask God to forgive us while we live with unforgiveness towards others. Why is that? Because God is concerned with reconciliation, with covenant, with us loving our neighbour as ourselves. Interestingly, this is the only part of the Lord's Prayer where Jesus amplifies his statement. He explains why we must pray about forgiveness; there are consequences if we refuse to offer it to each other.

Biblical reconciliation necessarily involves forgiveness. Reconciliation is the result of forgiveness. Reconciliation means that a relationship has broken down or been damaged. Somebody, through their actions, attitudes or words has caused estrangement and separation from somebody else. Hearts have turned away from each other and they need to be turned back to each other in reconciliation. In reconciliation, somebody asks for forgiveness and somebody grants it. Reconciliation turns hearts towards each other.

God's nature is to forgive sins: he is never reluctant to forgive when we repent and ask him to forgive. It is God's character to forgive; it demonstrates his love, grace and mercy:

If my people, who are called by my name, will humble themselves and pray and seek my face and turn from their wicked ways, then will I hear from heaven and will forgive their sin and will heal their land. (2Chronicles 7:14)

When you were dead in your sins and in the uncircumcision of your sinful nature, God made you alive with Christ. He forgave us all our sins, having cancelled the written code, with its regulations, that was against us and that stood opposed to us; he took it away, nailing it to the cross. (Colossians 2:13-14)

When God forgives he chooses not to remember our sins ever again. He will never call them to mind. In that sense he 'forgets'. The Bible says that when God forgives our sins he does not remember them anymore:

"This is the covenant I will make with the house of Israel after that time," declares Yahweh. "I will put my law in their minds and write it on their hearts. I will be their God, and they will be my people...For I will forgive their wickedness and will remember their sins no more." (Jeremiah 31:33-34)

Hebrews takes up this passage from Jeremiah twice (Hebrews 8:8-13; 10:16-18) to explain that this is the covenant we live in now as Christians. The New Covenant in Christ means that God has forgiven *all* our sins and no longer remembers them. They are gone! Does that mean our past sins are actually erased from God's memory? If that is the case then he does not know everything that has ever happened. Of course he can remember our sins; God has a perfect memory and perfect knowledge. He is all-knowing. Nothing goes out of his mind as if he suffers some form of divine amnesia. What it means is that God does not deal with us through the filter of our previous sinful life:

For as high as the heavens are above the earth, so great is his love for those who fear him. As far as the east is from the west, so far has he removed our transgressions from us. (Psalm 103:11-12)

Once he has forgiven us God chooses never to bring back up before us what we used to be or what we did. For him, it has gone and is no longer an issue. God does not see me as an ex-sinner; he sees me only as righteous and deals with me solely on the basis of who I am in Christ. When the Bible says that God will remember my sins no more, it means they are no longer a barrier between us. He will never raise them again, because they no longer exist. He will not even discuss them with me. If I were to bring up my sinful past life with him, his response would be, 'What are you talking about?'

It is the same if I sin as a believer. My new nature is to live to please my heavenly Father; it is not inevitable that I will sin. I do not face each new day with dread, worried about all the sins I might or might not commit during the day. I sin only when I choose to do so; when I allow the flesh to dominate. If I sin, I am always able to approach my Father in repentance. This is what happens when I do: *If we confess our sins he is faithful and just and will forgive us our sins* (1John 1:9). This is the power of God's forgiveness. He forgives swiftly and gladly; the result of his forgiveness is my reconciliation with him. Whatever it was in me that caused his displeasure, grief, even anger, is gone and forgotten. It is as if it never happened. God does not keep it in his back pocket and bring it out if I sin again, because: *Love keeps no record of wrongs* (1Corinthians 13:5).

The way God forgives us is exactly the way we forgive each other. Unforgiveness is a spiritual cancer that eats away at the hearts of people. Galatians 5:15 says: *If you keep on biting and devouring each other, watch out or you will be destroyed by each other.* Some are unwilling to forgive those who have done them harm, preferring to harbour bitterness and hatred (which often accompany unforgiveness) towards the person who mistreated them or sinned against them. Others say, 'I can forgive but I can't forget', meaning that they will always remember the harm done to them and will use it as a shield of protection or a weapon of revenge in the future. Neither of these ways is acceptable for Jesus' disciples. I am not downplaying some of the horrific things done to people. The appalling suffering by, and the unimaginable physical and psychological damage and abuse done to, innocent people is evil and, in many cases, too awful to imagine. Nevertheless, we are miraculously able to be those who live forgiven and forgiving, no matter what we have done to others or what others have done to us.

Jesus and the writers of the New Testament were well aware of the power of forgiveness and of the power of unforgiveness. Therefore, there is much emphasis on the necessity for us to always forgive one another:

> *As God's chosen people, holy and dearly loved, clothe yourselves with compassion, kindness, humility, gentleness and patience. Bear with each other and forgive whatever grievances you may have against one another. Forgive as the Lord forgave*

you. And over all these virtues put on love, which binds them all together in perfect unity. (Colossians 3:12-14)

"When you stand praying, if you hold anything against anyone, forgive him, so that your Father in heaven may forgive you your sins." (Mark 11:25)

"If your brother sins against you, rebuke him, and if he repents, forgive him." (Luke 17:3)

Jesus explained the importance of forgiveness in response to a question that Peter asked him:
"Lord, how many times shall I forgive my brother when he sins against me? Up to seven times?" Jesus answered, "I tell you, not seven times, but seventy times seven." (Matthew 18:21-22)

Peter thought he was being generous in his estimation. Jesus showed him he was completely wide of the mark. 'Seventy times seven' means there is no limit to the number of times you forgive somebody. Jesus then explained what he meant through the parable of the unmerciful servant. He was a man whose master forgave him a debt of millions of pounds, but who then immediately refused to forgive his fellow servant who owed him only a few hundred pounds (Matthew 18:21-35). The unmerciful servant was hauled back before his master who sent him to jail until he repaid the master all his own debt. The man's unwillingness to have mercy on his fellow servant and grant him forgiveness cost him his own forgiveness and freedom. Jesus warned: *"This is how my heavenly Father will treat each of you unless you forgive your brother from your heart"* (Matthew 18:35).

We must forgive as the Lord forgives us because we love in the same way that he loves. You cannot love like the Lord and not forgive like the Lord. There is a direct correlation between our forgiveness of others and the Lord's forgiveness of us. If we refuse to forgive those who sin against us, then the Lord will not forgive us. We can come to him and ask him to forgive us of our sins, but if we hold unforgiveness towards anybody in our hearts, he will not forgive us. He will say, 'Forgive that person and then I will forgive you.' We cannot expect God to behave in a manner that we refuse to behave in.

Forgiveness is so powerful it forgives even when people do not ask for it. Even when those who have done you wrong do not ask for forgiveness, you still forgive them. Your heart is so filled with love, grace and mercy that you live free by forgiving even those who never ask for it. The most famous example in the Word of God, of course, is that of Jesus. As he hung on the Cross, he said to his Father: *'Father, forgive them, for they don't know what they are doing'* (Luke 23:34). If ever anybody could justify a refusal to forgive, it was Jesus. He suffered and died as an innocent, sinless man, publicly abused, in the most unimaginable pain, completely alone.

Yet even here Jesus willingly forgave all those who slandered him, falsely accused him, beat him, robbed him and killed him. He died a free man.

Consider/Discuss
Do you need to forgive anybody?

Do you need to ask somebody's forgiveness?

TWENTY EIGHT

TESTING TIMES

*Do not lead us into temptation, but deliver us from evil.
(Matthew 6:13)*

Don't bring us to times of testing, but rescue us from the evil one. (Alternate translation)

Certain biblical passages stick in our minds once we learn them; that can sometimes mean we don't reflect on them sufficiently enough. I think this is one of those verses. Like countless others I learned the Lord's Prayer as a child; but for a long time this was one of the parts of the Masterplan which left me confused. Why would we ask God not to lead us into temptation, as if he would do such a thing as tempt us to sin? Why would God actively expose us to the possibility of sinning against him by tempting us to do wrong? It didn't make sense. I believe there is a simple answer: some English versions translate the verse inaccurately.

The word 'tempt' (*peirazō*) also means *to test, to make proof of, to prove, a trial*. It is translated in all these ways in the New Testament:

Test *yourselves to see if you are in the faith.
(2Corinthians 13:5)*

*Your fathers **tested** me, tried me and saw my works.
(Hebrews 3:9)*

*The **tempter** approached Jesus and said, 'If you are the Son of God, tell these stones to become bread.' (Matthew 4:3)*

*You rejoice in this, though now for a short time you have had to be distressed by various **trials**. (1Peter 1:6)*

> *Blessed is the man who perseveres under **trial**; for once he has been approved, he will receive the crown of life which the Lord has promised to those who love Him. Let no one say when he is **tempted**, "I am being **tempted** by God"; for God cannot be **tempted** by evil, and He Himself does not **tempt** anyone. (James 1:12-13)*

We see that the word is used both for tempting and for testing; the context is therefore vitally important in understanding which form of the word is meant. This is especially the case in the verse we are considering, because if we use the word 'tempt' to describe an act of God, we could land in all sorts of difficulties and error. And as we have just seen, God doesn't tempt anyone (James 1:12-13). God is a good God, and does only good. He is incapable of thinking anything evil, let alone doing anything to cause us to sin against him. The notion that he would purposely tempt us to sin against him and so incur his wrath and judgement is incorrect. If God were to behave like that it would make him evil, since he would be seen to entice us to disobey him. It would also put him in league with the tempter, his arch enemy the devil.

Therefore, when we come to a word in Scripture which can legitimately be translated in various ways, we have to take into account the person or circumstance mentioned in context with the word. We must apply what we know of that person from other passages in the Word of God; that will help to give us the correct meaning of the word in any particular verse. When we apply that rule we must conclude that this verse cannot mean that God leads us into temptation to cause us to sin against him. The second half of the verse confirms that: *'deliver us from the evil one'* - keep us from the power and influence of the enemy of our faith, the one who would do all in his evil ability to make us sin against God.

If God doesn't tempt us we are left with another question: does God test or prove us? Yes, he does. His tests or his proving of us aren't like exams in which we pass or fail; our heavenly Father is not trying to trip us up or catch us out. He is for us (Romans 8:31); nevertheless, he does prove or test us. These testings are the ways in which God from time to time acts in our lives to achieve his purpose in us. Sometimes we find him actively doing so in the Word of God, creating situations in which he proves his servants (see the example of Joseph in Psalm 105:17-19). At other times, such as the trials mentioned in 1Peter 1:6, which can happen just from life's circumstances, he uses them to prove us. We have to know the reality of Romans 8:28 - *we know that **all things** work together for the good of those who love God.* Any biblical character worth their salt was proved by God at some - or several points - in their lives.

One of the best known examples of God's proving is found in Genesis chapter 22, when God commanded Abraham to sacrifice Isaac as a burnt offering:

After these things God tested Abraham and said to him, 'Abraham!' 'Here I am,' he answered. 'Take your son, your only son, Isaac, whom you love, go to the land of Moriah, and offer him there as a burnt offering on one of the mountains I will tell you about.' (Genesis 22:1-2)

In each part of the story you will find that Abraham responded to God in exemplary fashion. God proved him, and Abraham proved something to himself: that he was a worshipper of God, that nothing and nobody would ever take God's supreme place in his life. God himself testified that Abraham was proved though this incident:

'Now I know that you fear God, since you have not withheld your only son from me.' (Genesis 22:12)

Lest we think that God only tests or proves us in challenging circumstances, he also proves us in the good times. God will even prove you in the blessing he bestows on you:

When you have eaten your fill, be sure to praise Yahweh your God for the good land he has given you. But that is the time to be careful! Beware that in your plenty you do not forget Yahweh your God and disobey his commands, regulations, and decrees that I am giving you today. For when you have become full and prosperous and have built fine homes to live in, and when your flocks and herds have become very large and your silver and gold have multiplied along with everything else, be careful! Do not become proud at that time and forget Yahweh your God, who rescued you from slavery in the land of Egypt. Do not forget that he led you through the great and terrifying wilderness with its poisonous snakes and scorpions, where it was so hot and dry. He gave you water from the rock! He fed you with manna in the wilderness, a food unknown to your ancestors. **He did this to humble you and test you for your own good.** *He did all this so you would never say to yourself, 'I have achieved this wealth with my own strength and energy.' Remember Yahweh your God. He is the one who gives you power to be successful, in order to fulfil the covenant he confirmed to your ancestors with an oath. (Deuteronomy 8:10-18)*

God warned his people about the prosperity they were about to enjoy, with a reminder of how and why he cared for them in the desert. He proved them in the wilderness and he will prove them now that they will have abundance. In effect he said to them, 'Good times are on you! When you are rich and have a wonderful house, and everything is going well in your life: remember me. I'm the One who enabled you to get there.' We could easily translate that into our lives: You have a good job? Your health is good? You've just received a promotion at work? You got that computer or watch you've always wanted? Your kids got into that school? You have more money now than you ever dreamed? You live in a lovely house in a great neighbourhood? You just received an unexpected bonus? The Lord is proving or testing you with that blessing: don't say that it was your own skill or hard work that got you there. It was God who enabled you to do all that; he is proving you to see if you still worship and serve him with the same passion as you did when you had little or nothing. Now you have more do you still need him? For example: if you have had a salary increase, has the tithe increased too? Are you giving more to the Lord in your offering? What effect has the testing of the Lord had on you?

God's ultimate purpose is not merely to bless you and make you happy; that is a self-centred way of looking at God. Some believe that God exists only to care for them and ensure that they never have a difficult day. If that's what you think God is like, you don't understand his love and grace, and you're in for a shock. God's ultimate purpose for you is to bring you to full maturity. He will do whatever is necessary within his holy and righteous ways to get you there. Part of that process is the proving of your faith, to see how genuine you really are:

> *In this you greatly rejoice, though now for a short time you have had to be distressed by various trials, so that the proof of your faith, being more precious than gold which is perishable, even though tested by fire, may be found to result in praise and glory and honour at the revelation of Jesus Christ. (1Peter 1:6-7)*

We don't live with a sense of fatalism, expecting trouble and testing all the time. That's why Jesus says we should pray to our heavenly Father about such things. We don't go looking for trials and tests; we live in victory over the evil one. It's somewhat like the situation Jesus faced in Gethsemane when he prayed:

> *'My Father: If it is possible, let this cup pass from me. Yet not as I will, but as you will.' (Matthew 26:39)*

He knew that he faced an incredible trial, one which his Father had planned for him from eternity. Jesus didn't relish what lay ahead, but neither was he looking for a way out. In his prayer he expressed his heart: 'I'm not looking forward to what lies ahead, but Father I know it's your will in order to achieve salvation for your people. Even though I face suffering and death I will do your will.' The New Testament says:

> *For the joy set before him he endured the cross, scorning its shame, and sat down at the right hand of the throne of God. (Hebrews 12:2)*

Jesus tells us we can talk to God in the secret place about these testing times when he proves us. We understand the ways of God and we see that they are opportunities to grow in faith; they are part of the maturing process. Our heavenly Father is at work in us.

Consider/Discuss
In what ways does God prove or test you?

How have these testing times changed you?

TWENTY NINE

KINGDOM - POWER - GLORY

*Yours is the kingdom and the power and the glory forever. Amen.
(Matthew 6:13)*

Jesus concludes his teaching on prayer in the secret place by drawing our attention to three things that have their source in our heavenly Father: the kingdom, the power and the glory. He reminds us that as we leave the secret place we should focus again on the same things as when we entered.

1. The Kingdom
We have mentioned the kingdom of God several times already, and we've discovered that it is a recurring theme throughout the Masterplan and the Bible as a whole. The kingdom is the rule and reign of God. We are born again into the kingdom. It belongs to the poor in spirit and to those who are persecuted for righteousness; it is also the first thing we pray about in the secret place. It's important that the kingdom is mentioned again at the end of the Lord's Prayer. The kingdom is the focus of a disciple's attention; later we will see that Jesus tells us to make the kingdom our priority, to keep seeking it first (Matthew 6:33). Therefore it must always be the focus of our prayer life so that we don't stray into concentrating on other things that could de-centralise or sideline the kingdom of God in our lives. The kingdom of God is all-encompassing; the church functions as it should only when it expresses the kingdom. That doesn't mean the church is irrelevant - far from it - the church is the instrument of the kingdom and manifests the kingdom on earth. A disciple who grasps the meaning of the kingdom of God and a church that lives for the kingdom will have an impact on this world that self-centred Christianity will never have. Recently I met a young man who had moved halfway across the world because the Holy Spirit began to envision him about the kingdom. When you see the kingdom - and

even more importantly, the King of the kingdom - you will do anything and go anywhere for Him.

2. The Power

Jesus promised us power - *dunamis* - the divine ability to live the life he expects of us and died and rose again to give us (Acts 1:8). The modern word *dynamite* comes from it, to explain the power that is in the explosive - it has the ability to change things completely. Unlike the man-made explosive, however, the power that Jesus talks of here is not destructive. The power is a Person: the Holy Spirit. When we consider the ability that the Holy Spirit possesses it's truly staggering: he created the universe, he raised Jesus from the dead, he transformed us from sinners to saints. Now that power is in us, because the Holy Spirit has come to live within us. All the ability that created the universe is in you, because the One who has all that power has made his home in you. The gifts of the Holy Spirit are manifestations of God's power. The kingdom of God is not only being righteous in the Holy Spirit (Romans 14:17), it's a kingdom of power, of demonstration (1Corinthians 4:20). Jesus not only taught about the kingdom of God, he also demonstrated it. He said: *'If I cast out demons by the Spirit of God, then the kingdom of God has come to you'* (Matthew 12:28). John Wimber used to say that the words of Jesus illuminate the kingdom, and the works of Jesus illustrate the kingdom. We need both these aspects of illumination and illustration to display the kingdom fully. Always bear in mind that whenever you lead somebody to Christ or lay hands on the sick you are illustrating the kingdom; you're making it visible in just the same way that Jesus did when he was on earth.

Equally important is the fruit of the Holy Spirit (Galatians 5:22-26); this is also the power of God working through us, producing the character of Jesus. Christians are the most powerful people on earth because the God of all power has chosen to live in us. We should always leave the secret place empowered. When we pray, 'Yours is the power', we remind ourselves of all the ability of God that is now in us and available to us to increase the kingdom.

3. The Glory

Glory is a word frequently used by Christians. Both the Hebrew and Greek words mean *heavy, weighty, to be laden down with wealth and great position.* It means to have the highest honour. When we speak of God's glory we are describing his essential 'God-ness' - he is uniquely glorious and majestic. His entire being shines with a pure and holy radiance. The glory of God is the tangible, demonstrable manifestation of his divine majesty. God alone is glorious; he doesn't share it with anybody or anything (Exodus 15:11; Isaiah 42:8).

The glory of God provokes awe and terror. In the Bible when God appears in his glory people often fall on their faces in worship and fear. They are completely overwhelmed by the glorious presence of God. Sometimes they are convinced they are going to die, because they have found themselves in the presence of the God of glory. For example, on the night Jesus was born:

There were shepherds living out in the fields nearby, keeping watch over their flocks at night. An angel of the Lord appeared to them, and the glory of the Lord shone around them, and they were terrified. (Luke 2:8-9)

Even though the glory of God provokes both awe and terror, it doesn't drive us away from God's presence. The glory of God has something about it that attracts us towards him like a divine magnet. We were created to fellowship with the God of glory, not to hide from him as Adam did after he had sinned. The glory of God tells us we can approach God, but should do so with reverent caution. When the Bible tells us we can come with absolute confidence into God's presence as God's children because of the blood of Jesus (Hebrews 10:19-22), we must never come flippantly or with casual familiarity. We come with faith and expectation; we approach him with full assurance of his welcoming arms. But we never come to him as equals; we come in reverence and awe. God is still a consuming fire (Hebrews 12:28-29). He is the glorious God.

When we leave the secret place of prayer we should always expect that time to have had an impact on us. Moses' face shone with a reflected glory when he spent time in God's presence (Exodus 34:29-35), but that radiance gradually faded after he left. However, the God of glory now lives within us so that we radiate his glory from within with an ever-increasing glory (2Corinthians 3:18). The glory of God within us doesn't fade away, it increases. Time in the secret place is vital in ensuring that we always behold the face of the God of glory, and demonstrate his glory to the world.

Consider/Discuss

What is it like to have the Holy Spirit who created the universe living in you?

How do you radiate the glory of God?

THIRTY

TRUE FASTING

Whenever you fast, don't be sad-faced like the hypocrites. For they make their faces unattractive so their fasting is obvious to people. I assure you: They've got their reward! But when you fast, put oil on your head, and wash your face, so that you don't show your fasting to people but to your Father who is in secret. And your Father who sees in secret will reward you. (Matthew 6:16-18)

This is the third occasion in the Masterplan where Jesus contrasts the hypocrite and the disciple. We have seen what Jesus expects of us regarding our giving and our prayer life; now he turns his attention to our fasting.

Jesus expects that his disciples will fast ('whenever you fast'), and that we will do so in a certain way. Fasting is common throughout the Word of God - people like Moses, Elijah, Esther, David, Anna, Paul - and of course Jesus himself - all fasted. Cities and entire nations fasted. Fasting has also been a constant feature of the church throughout its history. What is fasting? Simply: fasting is the deliberate abstention from food, and sometimes fluids, for spiritual purposes. Fasting isn't going on a hunger strike to try and twist God's arm or to convince him to act. Fasting is not dieting or de-toxing the body; nor is it self-denial or self-abasement to show God and others how spiritual we are (this is what Jesus condemns in this passage). Some say that one can fast from an activity - television, movies, or social media, for example. I understand what they mean by that and agree it is occasionally good to do such things. However, biblically, fasting is specifically to do with food and drink, the basic necessities of life.

Normally, fasting is abstaining from food, but not from water. Jesus fasted for 40 days (Luke 4:1-2); the Word of God says that during this time he didn't eat anything. We can assume from this that he continued to drink water. We sometimes see occasions where neither food nor liquids are consumed (Esther 4:16; Acts 9:9), but these are the exception. Occasionally people restricted or modified their food intake for a specific, spiritual purpose (Daniel 1:8-15; 10:2-3). Moses spent 40 days and nights with God on Mount Sinai, receiving the 10 Commandments (Exodus 34:28; Deuteronomy 9:9-18). During this time Moses neither ate bread nor drank water. We could call this a 'supernatural' fast.

The purpose of fasting is to set aside our legitimate bodily needs to pursue God; we fast unto the Lord to spend time with him. We might fast by forgoing food for a day or more, or just one meal during the day. The important thing to remember - and which Jesus reminds us in this passage - is that it's always done unto the Lord. There is no specific period for one to fast - it's done by the leading of the Holy Spirit. I have sometimes set apart some days for fasting only for the Holy Spirit to tell me to eat after one day. At other times I have set apart one day only for the Holy Spirit to lead me on to further time than originally planned. Fasting - like anything else - must never become legalistic or an attempt to become ascetic. That is of no value. If the Holy Spirit impresses on you to fast for one meal only, then do as he says. Fasting is not an external exercise, as the Pharisees had made it. Fasting is a spiritual discipline that one undergoes at the Holy Spirit's leading in order to do spiritual business with God.

The key in fasting is that the time one would usually spend eating is spent in prayer and/or the Word of God. It can even mean spending more time in the secret place. In fasting we don't carry on as normal during the times when we would be eating. We use that time instead for being with our heavenly Father. Many of the biblical examples show us that people ceased from other activities when fasting to concentrate on the matter in hand - deliverance from enemies, a prayer burden, wanting to receive further revelation and understanding, a major direction or decision, breakthrough, or simply to humble oneself. It can also be one of the triggers for revival. Fasting heightens our spiritual sensitivity and awareness; it enables us to focus on the matter in hand as we forsake legitimate bodily needs to pursue and seek our heavenly Father. Let me encourage you to search the Word of God for yourself to see the effects that fasting has on situations.

The point that Jesus makes is that when we fast, others should not be aware of it; we don't parade our spirituality by looking as if we're fasting or adopting a pseudo-spiritual demeanour. Like our giving, it's something done 'in secret'. Practically, that means we don't broadcast the fact that we are fasting - we just fast. If we are offered food during the fast we discreetly decline. Having said that, I did find myself in a situation when I was fasting and was offered a meal. The situation was such that a refusal would have been regarded by my host as the ultimate insult, so I accepted the kind offer and ate - as little as possible! Let me re-iterate: fasting is done in the Holy Spirit. Fasting is not a badge we wear to impress others. You might be fasting while carrying out your work; ensure that you are able to perform your duties for your employer properly if you are fasting. He pays your wages, so you must honour him. You might not be able to fast because of sickness, are pregnant or a nursing mother; or you are on medication that must be taken with food. The Lord always looks at your heart; never forget that. The main thing is that whatever we do, we do it unto the Lord with an attitude that doesn't draw attention to us, but only to him.

Consider/Discuss
How often do you fast?

How does fasting affect your spiritual awareness?

THIRTY ONE

YOU CAN'T TAKE IT WITH YOU

Don't collect for yourselves treasures on earth, where moth and rust destroy and where thieves break in and steal. But collect for yourself treasures in heaven, where neither moth nor rust destroys, and where thieves don't break in and steal. For where your treasure is, there your heart will be also. The eye is the lamp of the body. If your eye is good, your whole body will be full of light. But if your eye is bad, your whole body will be full of darkness. So if the light within you is darkness - how deep is that darkness! No one can be a slave of two masters, since he will hate one and love the other, or be devoted to one and despise the other. You cannot be slaves of God and of mammon. (Matthew 6:19-24)

Several times during the Masterplan Jesus pulls us right back to the core of his message: being his disciple is all about the condition of our spiritual hearts. It's about our priorities, about focussing on the right things, and not expending all our energy and resources on the temporary things of life.

Jesus does this again here. He lets us know, in no uncertain terms, that each of us faces a choice between two opposing ways of life - heavenly or earthly, the eternal or the temporal, God or Mammon. Jesus says we are defined by our choices; those choices are made from what we have decided is the most important thing in our lives. He calls it our treasure.

Treasure can be anything. It's what we dream about and what we spend our time and energy on. Our treasure is what we are enthusiastic and excited about. It's what sets our pulse racing. Our treasure determines how and where we spend - or don't spend - our money. It's what we value the most, what consumes us. It can be a career; a sport or hobby; it can be family or personal ambition; it can be another person or material possessions. Our treasure is our abiding passion; it takes priority over everything and everyone else.

Our treasure is what gets us up in the morning and keeps us going. Whatever our treasure is, it controls us, because we value that treasure more than anything else. In fact, our treasure owns us; Jesus says we are slaves to our treasure. We could even say our treasure is what we worship; we see more worth in it than in anything else.

Jesus warns us that anything we treasure which is not 'heavenly' is ultimately a waste of time and energy; it won't stand the ultimate test of judgement in the age to come. This takes us back to the opening of the Lord's Prayer: 'your kingdom come - your will be done on earth as it is in heaven.' The way we live here on earth determines our rewards and responsibilities in the age to come - many of Jesus' parables speak about this. In fact, he referred to the kingdom of God as treasure (Matthew 13:44). Therefore we need to be aware that what we treasure in life and pour our energies into while we are here will be used to judge us when we get to heaven. We are to 'store up treasures in heaven', we are to focus our lives on the heavenly kingdom of God. That's what Paul meant in 1Corinthians 3:12-15 when he compared how we spend our lives to gold, silver, costly stones, or wood, hay and straw. When God's fire of judgement on our lives tests our values and actions - our treasure - what will remain? It's vital, therefore, that we live with an eternal perspective. That doesn't mean we can't enjoy the natural things of life, as long as they're not unrighteous; but Jesus emphasises that he doesn't want anything to replace God in our lives. If anything does then it becomes our god, our treasure. God doesn't mind us owning things: he doesn't want things owning us.

In verses 22 and 23 Jesus makes his teaching practical by warning us to be aware of the power of our eyes for good and evil. We must have a single, focussed, good eye. In chapter 5:27 he already spoke of this when talking about personal morality; now he says we must take care of the relationship between our heart and our eyes. We might see something that we'd like and be attracted by it and then want it until we find that it becomes all consuming - our treasure. It can be material objects; it can be a lifestyle we want to live, a place we want to go, a home we want to own, a person we'd like to be. Advertisers understand the power of our senses, especially our sight: why do you think they spend so much money convincing you to buy their products? Jesus said the eye is the lamp of the body (verse 22);

keep it good by ensuring the values of your heart rule what you see, and not the other way round. Remember too what Jesus said elsewhere: *'A man's life does not consist in the abundance of his possessions'* (Luke 12:15). The Word of God talks about having a vision - what we see - and what keeps us going. Paul said he was obedient to the heavenly vision (Acts 26:19) - his heart and his eye were focussed on the same thing. You can't close your physical eyes to all the world has to offer, but your spiritual eyes will help you see their true value. Don't let them own you.

In one of the most dramatic statements in the Gospels, Jesus declares that when all is said and done, we all serve only one Master. In this instance he contrasts God and Mammon. The word that Jesus uses here is not the normal word for money; he uses *mamōnas* which comes from a term meaning *the treasure we put our trust in*. It describes the spirit or controlling power behind the love of money, the dominating power that money can have over us if we love it and chase after it. We have already established that money itself is neutral; but the love of money will control and eventually destroy you. Later in Matthew's Gospel, Jesus applied this part of the Masterplan when he met the rich young ruler (Matthew 19:16-22). The man was prepared to be a disciple of Jesus until Jesus put his finger on the very issue that controlled him. He had another treasure: Mammon. In fact, he'd broken the very first commandment - money was his god and he wasn't going to give that god up for Jesus. So Jesus let him go. Jesus offered him 'treasure in heaven' (Matthew 19:21); but the young man already had his treasure on earth, and one day it would be destroyed by 'moths and rust' or 'thieves would break in and steal it'. He made the wrong choice; we never hear of him again.

Consider/Discuss
What is your treasure?

What 'treasures' are you storing in heaven?

THIRTY TWO

PERSPECTIVES AND PRIORITIES

This is why I tell you: Don't worry about your life, what you will eat or what you will drink; or about your body, what you will wear. Isn't life more than food and the body more than clothing? Look at the birds of the sky: They don't sow or reap or gather into barns, yet your heavenly Father feeds them. Aren't you worth more than they? Can any of you add a single inch to his height by worrying? And why do you worry about clothes? Learn how the wildflowers of the field grow: they don't labour or spin thread. Yet I tell you that not even Solomon in all his splendour was adorned like one of these! If that's how God clothes the grass of the field, which is here today and thrown into the furnace tomorrow, won't He do much more for you - you of little faith? So don't worry, saying, 'What will we eat?' or 'What will we drink?' or 'What will we wear?' For the idolaters eagerly seek all these things, and your heavenly Father knows that you need them. But seek first the kingdom of God and His righteousness, and all these things will be provided for you. Therefore don't worry about tomorrow, because tomorrow will worry about itself. Each day has enough trouble of its own.
(Matthew 6:25-34)

Jesus is approaching the final parts of the Masterplan. In view of all that he has presented, which is a radical way of life to say the least, he now says: 'I don't want you to worry about anything.' Worry must not be a feature of our lives as disciples; that's why in our family, my wife Dianne has a rule - no worrying! Admittedly, I have not always been successful in living free from worry, but having the instruction of Jesus, the help of the Holy Spirit and the encouragement of my wife and children has been a tremendous blessing! We have faced some enormous challenges over the years regarding health, finances, family, careers, disappointments and deferred hopes. In all those times the absence of worry and the presence of faith in God has enabled us to overcome seemingly insurmountable obstacles.

The word used for 'worry' here and elsewhere in the New Testament means *to be pulled in opposite directions, to be pulled apart, to be pulled to pieces.* It's a destructive term, and it describes worry perfectly. Worry is a destroyer. Worry can be anything from a general negative disposition to an acute, overwhelming anxiety which cripples a person spiritually, mentally, and physically. Jesus doesn't diminish the power of worrying; he knows how destructive it can be in our lives. He also knows that worry doesn't actually change anything - it won't add one centimetre to your height or one second to your life. In that one comment Jesus reveals the utter futility of worrying - the only effect it has is on the one who worries. And its effect is not good. Corrie Ten Boom said: 'Worry doesn't rob tomorrow of its sorrow, it empties today of its strength.' Worry has a debilitating power; worry paralyses and stifles initiative. Worry makes us doubt and fear. Worry will make us sick. Worry destroys faith. Fear is the driving force behind worry; fear stalks the worrier at every turn. The one who worries is controlled by fear, to whatever degree. Fear does not come from God; the New Testament says that we have not received a spirit of fearfulness (2Timothy 1:7). This New Testament term means *to be driven by fear.* On the contrary, we have received the Holy Spirit of power, love and a sound mind. That's why Jesus tells us not to worry (elsewhere he teaches us to actively forbid our hearts to be troubled - John 14:1). He wants us to live in the power of the Holy Spirit, that is our inheritance and birthright as children of God. He asserts that a life of worry and anxiety must not be present in his disciples, so he gives us a fourfold remedy.

The *first* part of the remedy is simply to look; to open our physical eyes to the things around us. Many of our worries are to do with the everyday things - what we eat and drink, our health and physical condition, the clothes we wear, our jobs. These are the ordinary and necessary things of everyday life. How do you prevent yourself worrying about such things? By looking! Jesus says, 'Look at the birds, look at the flowers, look at the grass.' Is he being literal? Yes he is. He tells us to get a proper sense of perspective; take time to look at the birds as they feed on grubs and seeds, as they peck at the ground. God is feeding them. Look at that beautiful rose or dahlia. It's adorned by God and it looks fabulous. Look at the grass, beautiful and lush: God clothes it. The grass will be gone tomorrow; the flowers will fade and die. Yet God cares for them. How much more does he care for you?

The creation has a purpose - to show you what your heavenly Father is like and how he cares for you. The secularist, atheistic drive to separate the creation from its Creator is having a disastrous effect on humanity's sense of spiritual perception and subsequent wholeness. The creation exists to display the glory of God and he uses it to speak to us. Maybe right now, you need to walk away from this book and sit in the garden or the park and look around you. Allow the Holy Spirit to speak to you.

The *second* part of Jesus' remedy for worry is to have faith in God. Faith is simple: it's a matter of believing what somebody tells you, with no doubt at all. You choose to believe the words you hear. Faith is not hard; it's a gift of God (Ephesians 2:8). It's also a gift of the Holy Spirit (1Corinthians 12:9). Faith and worry are mutually exclusive, they are totally incompatible. You can either have faith or you can worry; you can't do both! God designed you to live by faith in him. I use a simple formula for faith: God said it - I believe it - that settles it. For me faith is making the choice to believe what God says, no matter what circumstances might militate against his words. I trust his integrity; I believe he always speaks the truth; I am convinced that what he says will come to pass. That's faith.

The *third* part is to speak correctly. Jesus states: 'Don't worry, *saying...*' The tongue has the power of life and death (Proverbs 18:21); our words have creative or destructive power. Jesus says elsewhere (Matthew 12:33-37), that whatever is in our heart - what we have put there by faith - will come out in our words. I have written and spoken extensively over many years about the power of our words; faith is to do with hearing and speaking words that we have chosen to believe. We are saved by believing and by speaking agreement with what we have heard (Romans 10:9-10). The Word of God is full of instructions on the importance of speaking properly. Speak faith, don't speak worry; speaking worry will take you on a downward spiral. Agree with what the Word of God says: your heavenly Father knows what you need (verse 32). You will rise or sink to the level of your speaking, so make it a habit to speak agreement with what God says. Faith speaks: and faith speaks faith!

The *fourth* ingredient is to change priorities - to seek the kingdom of God and his righteousness. This takes us back to the beginning of the Masterplan, to the poor in spirit: those who are utterly dependent on God for everything. Theirs is the kingdom of God. Jesus tells us to take our eyes off our own needs and concerns and to focus instead on the kingdom of God, to 'make the kingdom of God our priority,' as the New Living Translation puts it. Yes, we need the everyday things of life - food, clothes, health, homes, money, jobs. But they must not be our priority; Jesus says that if we make the kingdom of God our priority then God will take care of us, he will provide for us, he will look after us. He will feed and clothe us, he will ensure we have all that we need. We do what he says and he does what he says. That's the loving care of a sovereign God: he says that if we utterly devote ourselves to him - which is the essence of discipleship - he will be faithful and will look after us. That means we have no fear of tomorrow or the future at all; God has it all under control. Once we make the kingdom of God our priority everything else falls into place. We have the proper perspective on life in all its aspects once we turn our focus from them to the kingdom of God. Our spiritual eyes are concentrated on the rule and reign of God over all, on his kingdom purpose, on Jesus the King of the kingdom, on our citizenship of the kingdom, on the power of the kingdom, on the Gospel of the kingdom being preached throughout the world. Once you embrace the kingdom of God life makes perfect sense.

Consider/Discuss
What causes you to worry?

When you look at God's creation, what does it say to you?

How do you keep the kingdom of God as your priority?

THIRTY THREE

SPECKS AND LOGS

Do not judge, so that you won't be judged. For with the judgment you judge, you will be judged, and with the measure you measure, it will be measured to you. Why do you look at the speck in your brother's eye but don't notice the log in your own eye? Or how can you say to your brother, 'Let me take the speck out of your eye,' and look, there's a log in your eye? Hypocrite! First take the log out of your eye, and then you will see clearly to take the speck out of your brother's eye. (Matthew 7:1-5)

It's sad that this section of the Masterplan is often taken entirely out of context by those so-called Christians who want to justify their ungodly way of life. They use these verses to excuse the fact that they don't want to be accountable to anybody. They want to live an independent life, unaccountable to other Christians and Christian leaders. That is a denial of the very essence of Christianity, which by its very nature is corporate. As we've already mentioned, all the images of the church in the New Testament, not forgetting those of the people of God in the Old Testament, are corporate and communal. The church is the Body of Christ, not a loose collection of isolated individuals (1Corinthians 12:12-27). We are the covenant community of God.

These words of Jesus have been thrown at me on several occasions by those ostensibly under my care, when, as their pastor, I've approached them regarding something contrary to the Scriptures in their walk with God. 'Who are you to judge me?' 'Nobody tells me what to do.' 'Who do you think you are?' 'God is my judge and I answer only to him.' 'The Bible says don't judge others.' Such conversations, if conversations we can call them, have never had a happy outcome. I admit that sometimes my timing and attitude didn't help; nevertheless these incidents always exposed an undercurrent of resistance to correction and sometimes revealed downright rebellion against authority.

If Jesus meant here that we should never judge each other then he contradicts himself, which he clearly doesn't! As we've already discovered, in Matthew 5:21-24 he teaches us how to respond to each other when there is conflict between believers. In Matthew 18:15-17 he specifically sets out the way in which we are obliged to deal with fellow Christians when they sin against us. Nowhere does he say, 'Say nothing, keep yourself to yourself, it's not your place to judge the actions and attitudes of others.' Quite the contrary: and the rest of the New Testament is equally strong in presenting the corporate responsibility of the church in making proper spiritual judgements about each other (read 1Corinthians chapter 3 for example). We are our brother's keeper.

We must read this entire section of the Masterplan to understand what Jesus is teaching us here. When we do that, it's clear. He is warning us about hypocrisy and double standards; he is not telling us to avoid making judgements. He puts his finger on the way we behave towards each other, specifically regarding our responsibility for each other's spiritual welfare. The practical example Jesus uses explains the first sentence: you must expect others to apply the same judgments and standards to you as you apply to others. Live by the standards you expect of others. The key is in the words *'first...then'* - before you try to address the fault or lack in somebody else (a 'speck'), make sure that the same fault or lack isn't present in you too as a 'log' (on an even bigger scale). Jesus' teaching here is another aspect of the Royal Law: Love your neighbour as yourself. Treat others the way you want them to treat you; don't demand from others what you're not prepared to do yourself. Don't be critical and judgmental of others when you behave the same as, or even worse than them. Before you try to sort others out, sort yourself out. In fact, don't try and sort people out at all. Armchair critics beware!

If I may speak as somebody who has had the privilege of leading God's people. I can't expect those under my care to live in a way that I'm not prepared to live myself. If I teach them to be good husbands and fathers, then I have to ensure that I too am a good husband and father. If I teach them to live by faith, then I live by faith. If I exhort them to be generous, then I too am generous. If I teach them not to

gossip, I don't gossip. If I teach them to exercise the gifts of the Holy Spirit, I exercise the gifts of the Holy Spirit. I not only practise what I preach: I preach what I practise. This is what Paul taught Timothy about leadership:
> *You should be an example for the believers in speech, in conduct, in love, in faith, in purity. (1Timothy 4:12)*

Note that Jesus not only uses the word 'judge', he also uses the word 'measure'. This is a very important New Testament term and occurs for example in Ephesians 4:11-13:
> *And he [the ascended Christ] personally gave some to be apostles, some prophets, some evangelists, some pastors and teachers, for the equipping of the saints in the work of service, to build up the body of Christ, until we all reach oneness in the faith and in the knowledge of God's Son, growing into a mature man with a stature <u>measured</u> by Christ's fullness.*

This passage describes the task of the Ephesians 4 gifts: to bring the church to maturity and oneness in the faith and in the knowledge of God's Son. What is the maturity and stature required to reach that? It's the *measure* of Christ's fullness; the same word that Jesus uses here in Matthew 7:2. The word is *metron*, meaning *a standard, or the basis for determining what is fair or sufficient*. A standard was the controlling factor by which things were determined to be correct. Jesus is the perfect standard, the measure, by which we determine everything. Our maturity is to attain to all he expects of us. Jesus is the perfect standard by which we measure everything, first of all ourselves, then one another as the body of Christ.

If we adopt this attitude and see judgement in that light, instead of being critical and judgmental of others, we will see people as Christ sees them, we will see Christ in them, we will love them as ourselves. Then we will be able to help each other, and when and where necessary, correct and encourage each other towards our ultimate maturity in Christ. We will also be willing to receive judgement and correction from our brothers and sisters so we can achieve such maturity. Personally, this means that I will always judge and measure myself against the standard of Jesus;

consequently that will determine how I judge and measure everybody else too.

Consider/Discuss
How do you like others to treat you?

How accountable are you to your leaders and to your fellow believers?

THIRTY FOUR

DOGS AND PIGS

Don't give what is holy to dogs or toss your pearls before pigs, or they will trample them with their feet, turn, and tear you to pieces. (Matthew 7:6)

At first glance this verse seems to stand in isolation from what precedes and follows it. On closer observation it relates very much to what Jesus has been saying about judgement and judging each other. Here he develops that theme. Jesus has taught us not to be judgemental in our attitudes; but that's only one side of the coin. Now he tells us that we must also be wise and discerning in the way we relate to others. He says a similar thing later in Matthew's Gospel when he sends out the disciples on their first mission without him:

'I'm sending you out like sheep among wolves. Therefore be as shrewd as serpents and harmless as doves.' (Matthew 10:16)

Jesus uses terminology that would make his immediate hearers recoil or cringe: he speaks about dogs and pigs. Unlike today in western cultures, dogs were not regarded as precious family members, doted on and pampered with the finest foods. They were regarded as dirty scavengers which fed on scraps and leftovers. They even ate human remains (1Kings 21:23-24; Psalm 68:23). Jesus also used this graphic imagery in his conversation with the Canaanite woman in Matthew 15:26-28 to provoke a faith response from her. Pigs were unclean animals; Jews were forbidden to eat any part of the pig or even keep them. When Jesus describes certain people as dogs and pigs, the graphic nature of his language would catch his hearers' attention: holy/pearls versus dogs/pigs. We are left with two questions: What is holy/pearl? Who are the dogs/pigs?

Everything to do with God is by its very nature holy. Remember how Jesus introduced prayer in the secret place: *'Our Father in heaven, your name be honoured as holy.'* God's holiness describes his total otherness: he is infinitely and morally pure or righteous. God doesn't have to attain a standard of holiness or righteousness: he *is* the standard by which everything else is measured. He alone is holy (Revelation 15:4). When we are born again we become holy: the word 'saint' in the New Testament is 'holy one' (Philippians 1:1). We are new creations in Christ (2Corinthians 5:17) who partake of the divine nature (2Peter 1:4). Jesus' disciples are holy people who represent a holy God to an unholy world. The things that we believe and practise are consequently holy because they demonstrate something of the nature of the holy God. They should be handled with reverence and respect; they are not playthings. They belong to God and reveal him. They all represent in some way what God is like. If we see things like the Cross, water baptism, baptism in the Holy Spirit, gifts of the Holy Spirit, breaking bread, tithing, worship, the blood of Jesus, the Word of God, marriage, the church, the kingdom of God, for what they really are, then our sensitivity to the holy God is greatly increased.

Holy things are therefore precious - they are like pearls. Jesus described the kingdom of God as a priceless pearl:

> *The kingdom of heaven is like a merchant in search of fine pearls. When he found one priceless pearl, he went and sold everything he had, and bought it. (Matthew 13:45-46)*

This is a beautiful illustration of the kingdom of God; it's like a priceless pearl. Somebody sold everything they had in order to obtain it. What makes the kingdom of God so priceless, so precious? It's the kingdom *of God* - of the holy God, and Jesus Christ is the King of that holy, precious, priceless kingdom. Everything to do with the kingdom is holy, priceless, precious, because it's to do with God. When we realise that we will careful how we behave in it; how and when we present it - and to whom we present it.

Who are the dogs/pigs? They are those who trample the holy and precious things of God underfoot, and then turn on the subjects of the kingdom. These can be certain unbelievers who are particularly aggressive and mocking towards Christianity. They deliberately set themselves up to offend Christians and to insult God. They especially target Jesus with their demeaning, blasphemous humour and hatred. However, dogs/pigs can sadly also be those who call themselves believers but who act like unbelievers - they give Christianity a bad name. Sadly there are those who describe themselves as Christians who live like atheists - they live like God doesn't exist. Their lives reflect negatively on Jesus. The Word of God acknowledges such people; in Proverbs it calls them fools or mockers. We are told how to behave towards such people:

Don't rebuke a mocker, or he will hate you; rebuke a wise man and he will love you. (Proverbs 9:8)

Don't answer a fool according to his foolishness, or he'll become wise in own eyes. (Proverbs 26:4)

This is where the disciple needs the leading of the Holy Spirit: you have to know what to say or not to say in every conversation, with all kinds of people. You have to face the fact that sometimes you will be dealing with dogs/pigs - those who will utterly devalue and sneer at your holy pearl - and you will have to decide that they are not worthy to hear what you have to say. You're not being judgmental; however, you are making a spiritual judgement. You're in good company; Jesus did the same with Herod at his trial. Despite Herod's questions Jesus refused to answer him; he said nothing (Luke 23:6-12). Jesus refused to offer a priceless pearl to this 'pig.' Proverbs also says:

Answer a fool according to his foolishness; or he'll become wise in his own eyes. (Proverbs 26:5)

A contradiction? No, of course not. The Word of God is reminding us not to make a law out of a principle. There will be times when the Holy Spirit will lead you to offer your precious, holy pearl, even though your hearers will refuse it and throw it back in your face. This happened at Pentecost: some of the observers sneered at the 120 men and women filled with the Holy Spirit and accused them of being drunk (Acts 2:13). They were behaving like 'dogs/pigs'. Jesus encountered the same with the religious leaders of the day. Sometimes he ignored them, at other times he turned their arrogance back on them and humiliated them in the eyes of ordinary people. He didn't have any qualms about doing so.

I am conscious that to write in this way of certain people being 'dogs/pigs' could be construed as being 'politically incorrect' and even insulting: I suppose that's true. But that's what Jesus does here. That is why what he has warned us about being judgmental in the previous verses is so important; his disciples are not to be arrogant, proud and dismissive. We must not become 'dogs/pigs'. Instead, we must be spiritually aware, and realise that the things of the kingdom of God are holy and precious. They must be handled correctly and demonstrated properly.

Consider/Discuss
What aspects of being a Christian are your pearls?

How do you respond when people act like dogs/pigs towards you?

THIRTY FIVE

KEEP ON KEEPING ON

Keep asking, and it will keep being given to you. Keep seeking, and you will keep finding. Keep knocking, and the door will keep being opened to you. For everyone who asks receives, and the one who searches finds, and to the one who knocks, the door will be opened. What man among you, if his son asks for bread, will give him a stone? Or if he asks for a fish will give him a snake? If you then, who are evil, know how to give good things to your children, how much more will your Father in heaven give good things to those who ask him! (Matthew 7:7-11)

As he approaches the climax of the Masterplan, Jesus exhorts us to keep on keeping on; to have an attitude of consistent perseverance. He urges us to keep on asking God, to keep on seeking him and to keep on knocking at his door. We don't lounge around, snoozing on the sofa of passivity, expecting God to do everything for us. It's true that he lives his life in us through the Holy Spirit; but we are active participants in that life. Neither do we have to sweat and strain, haranguing and cajoling God through our best efforts. We are not beggars; we are sons of God. Jesus isn't telling us to wear ourselves out trying to twist God's arm; rather, he shows us something of the nature of God and how we relate to him as his children.

Jesus assures us that our asking, seeking and knocking are never in vain. He promises that we will receive, we will find, and doors will be opened. First of all he uses the example of natural fathers: which of us would give our son a doll if he asked us for a football? That would be cruel and vindictive; it would destroy our son's confidence and trust in us as a father. I am a father; when my children were little and I was away from them, I always made sure that I brought them back a gift - one that they would be thrilled to receive. It didn't have to be expensive; but I knew what my kids liked and bought accordingly.

Jesus calls us earthly fathers 'evil' - once again he employs hyperbole to compare us with God the Father, whom he describes as a 'how much more Father'. God isn't like an early father only a million times better; he's a different kind of Father altogether. If we earthly fathers know how to treat our children, imagine how much more - infinitely more - God our Father will treat his children. God isn't going to play tricks on us or give us things that will harm us or disappoint us. He knows what is best for us and he knows what we can handle and when we can handle it. He knows what is for our benefit and what is not; he knows what we can be entrusted with. Everything God does to us and with us as our Father is aimed to bring us to maturity as his sons and further the kingdom of God. He is good and kind; he is also wise. This passage doesn't mean that we just decide what we want and then pummel God into submission until he gives in to us. Jesus made that clear in the parable of the persistent widow (Luke 18:1-8); we need to pray and 'not become discouraged' about things like justice and righteousness, not our personal preferences or selfish desires.

The New Testament constantly exhorts us to persevere in our faith. Among other things perseverance produces character (Romans 5:3-4). I'm sure you've discovered that sometimes you pray and receive the answer immediately. However, at other times you have to keep going, you have to persist, you have to keep on seeking, asking and knocking. I don't know why this is so. I do know that at just the right time God acts. He always does everything right on time - his time. I'm learning that God's perfect timing is also mine. In those seasons when I have to keep on asking, seeking and knocking I learn more about God's faithfulness, that I mustn't get frustrated, and to live increasingly according to his promises. It also builds tenacity into my character.

It's unfortunate that some translations use the phrase 'good things' in verse 11. The text literally says *'he will give good'* - that puts a different slant on Jesus' words. He's already told us in chapter 6 not to worry about things, but to seek the kingdom of God. He says here that we should continue to seek (the same word is used as in Matthew 6:33). What are we to keep on seeking? The kingdom of God, not 'things.' Luke's account of this passage adds something of utmost importance; in Luke 11:13 Jesus says our heavenly Father *'will give the Holy Spirit to those who ask him'*. This lifts our asking, seeking and knocking to a whole different level, way beyond ourselves. We already know that God will provide what we need, and it's right that we persevere in our prayers regarding those needs (our 'daily bread'). However, our asking, seeking and knocking must also involve growing in our relationship with the Holy Spirit, and our subsequent ongoing effectiveness as Jesus' disciples. This constant asking, seeking and knocking ensures that we are always growing in the Holy Spirit - in his power, anointing, gifts and fruit. Even though we have the Holy Spirit in us we constantly grow in our fellowship with him. We also increase in stature as sons of God; we increase in our revelation of the kingdom of God; we increase in our intimacy with our heavenly Father; we increase in our effectiveness as disciples of the Lord Jesus Christ. We keep on keeping on.

Consider/Discuss
What are you seeking, asking and knocking for at the moment?

What does perseverance do for you?

Are you able to gauge areas of your life where you are increasing?

THIRTY SIX

THE GOLDEN RULE

Therefore, whatever you want others to do for you, do also the same for them - this is the Law and the Prophets. (Matthew 7:12)

It could be all too easy in reading the Masterplan to skim over this sentence. It comes at the end of a section and Jesus has a few more things left to say to us before he concludes. We could read it quickly and assume he's just telling us to be nice to people, as he moves on to the next big topic. The fact is that this sentence is one of the most significant in the Masterplan; I venture to say it's one of the most important in the entire New Testament.

Jesus refers to the Law and the Prophets. By this he means the Old Testament. A later incident in Jesus' ministry throws more light on what he tells us here. He was asked one of the most important questions anybody ever asked him:

An expert in the law tested Jesus with this question: "Teacher, which is the greatest commandment in the Law?" Jesus replied: "'Love the Lord your God with all your heart and with all your soul and with all your mind.' This is the first and greatest commandment. And the second is like it: 'Love your neighbour as yourself.' All the Law and the Prophets hang on these two commandments." (Matthew 22:35-40)

Jesus said that the Old Testament is essentially all about loving God, and loving our neighbour as ourselves. Jesus' questioner was concerned about doing the right thing, about keeping the commandments. He thought that doing what was right would make him right with God. That is still a common misunderstanding - that getting right with God is all about doing the right things. As E. Stanley Jones pointed out: 'The kingdom of God is concerned with what you are. The kingdoms of this world are concerned with what you do.' Jesus was concerned about *being* right, about who and what

we *are*. To demonstrate this he went to the Law of Moses (the first five books of the Old Testament), and brought it down to two statements. That is why Jesus' reply to the question was amazing. Contrary to the questioner's expectation, he made no reference to the 10 Commandments. Instead, Jesus referred to this passage:
> *Hear, O Israel: Yahweh our God, Yahweh is one. Love Yahweh your God with all your heart and with all your soul and with all your strength. These commandments that I give you today are to be upon your hearts. (Deuteronomy 6:4-6)*

Verse four says that there is only one God. That is the basis of the 10 Commandments: *You will have no other gods besides me* (Exodus 20:3). We are to worship and love this one God with all that we are. Verse six tells us that God's intention for his Law is that it will be written on our hearts. It is to be internalised within us in a love relationship with God. It was never destined to remain an external set of regulations, set on tablets of stone. It was given to be written on the 'tablet' of the heart. Jesus said the greatest commandment is that we love God with all that we are. Then he quoted a verse from Leviticus:
> *Do not seek revenge or bear a grudge against one of your people, but love your neighbour as yourself. I am Yahweh. (Leviticus 19:18)*

Jesus used this verse to explain the real meaning of all the other laws, and the practical outworking and proof of our love for God: love your neighbour as yourself. Jesus put these two statements together: love God with all your heart, and love your neighbour as yourself. The way we behave towards others is directly linked to how we love God and how we see ourselves. Let's remind ourselves of what Jesus said in the Masterplan:
> *In everything, do to others what you would have them do to you, for this sums up the Law and the Prophets. (Matthew 7:12)*

This is often called the Golden Rule. Even non-Christian philosophers agree that this is the ideal way to live. However, outside of a relationship with God through Jesus, it is impossible. Jesus said that treating others in the way that you would like them to treat you fulfils the Greatest Commandment. Behave towards others in the same way you would like them to behave towards you. Treat people the same way you like to be treated. The entire Old Testament is about this. Our love for God is not theoretical; it is intensely practical. How we treat other people really matters. It is the proof of our love for God. This theme runs through the New Testament:

Love does no harm to its neighbour. Therefore love is the fulfilment of the law. (Romans 13:10)

The entire law is summed up in a single command: 'Love your neighbour as yourself'. (Galatians 5:14)

If you really keep the royal law found in Scripture, 'Love your neighbour as yourself,' you are doing right. (James 2:8)

Later, in one of his most explosive teachings, Jesus set the pattern that would authenticate the church's Gospel message to the world. He talked about our love for each other and its consequent impact on the world: *'By this all men will know that you are my disciples: if you love one another'* (John 13:35). Jesus said that what will convince the world of his claims to be the Lord and Saviour of the world, and of the authenticity of our message, would not only be the power of our preaching, signs and wonders, good works, mission strategies and the many other things that comprise our Gospel. The one thing that will convince the world more than anything else will be the fact that we as his disciples love one another with the same love that God has for us.

However, God's love is not limited to Christians. He loves people. We do not limit our love only to our fellow brothers and sisters in Christ. It's true that in the church the love of God is expressed to each other in a special way. But that love also overflows to the world. We love all people with the love of God. Even though the church stands in stark contrast to the world and refuses to accept its values, the church's attitude to the world is always one of love and hope. God the Father did not send Jesus into the world to condemn it, but to save the world (John 3:17). Our attitude to the world is, therefore, *never* condemnatory but at all times redemptive. It is inevitable that our lifestyle and message will challenge and confront the world. We will make the world uncomfortable and angry, and by the very nature of who we are we will even sometimes cause people to hate us and to be hostile towards us (we discovered that in the Beatitudes). It is the nature of the Gospel of the kingdom to do that – it is offensive to the sinner (Galatians 5:11). Nevertheless, Jesus' disciples are radical in their love for sinners as well as in their fierce, uncompromising stand for the glory of Jesus. Our mission is to convey the love of God to his world and so establish his status quo, his kingdom. God's love is the motivation for our mission. Our love for God and our love for his world, therefore, are not mutually exclusive. We love God passionately and we love his world with the same passion as he does. Jesus loved people, all kinds of people. He mixed with prostitutes, lepers, political zealots and collaborators, business people, home-makers, children, farmers, soldiers, fishermen, the poor, and the social and political elite. He loved them all. It is true that not all of them reciprocated that love, but that was not the point. Jesus loved people unconditionally. The old adage is true: God loves sinners but hates sin. We hate what people are – they are sinners. Nevertheless, we love them even though they are sinners. That is why Jesus said this is the Greatest Commandment, because only God loves like that. In Christ, so do we.

Consider/Discuss
'Love your neighbour as yourself' - how do you see yourself?

Are there certain kinds of people you find it difficult to love?

THIRTY SEVEN

GATES AND ROADS

Enter through the narrow gate. For the gate is wide and the road is broad that leads to destruction, and there are many who go through it. How narrow is the gate and confined the road that leads to life, and few find it. (Matthew 7:13-14)

At the close of the Masterplan Jesus makes four graphic statements. Each of them contains warnings and commands. He leaves us with no illusions about the seriousness of being his disciple, and the consequences of rejecting him as Lord and King.

In the first of these statements Jesus uses another illustration that his hearers would identify with very easily. He speaks about gates: not the ornate kind that grand houses have or those of the picket fence variety, but about city gates. His audience went through them every time they entered or left a city. Many of us will have seen movies where an army was trying to get into a city being defended by its inhabitants. The easiest way to get into the city was through the gates; hence they were always heavily defended. Ancient cities were surrounded by walls and had gates to enter and exit by. A city wouldn't have lots of gates, just one or two, depending on the size of the city. This was because the gates were the most vulnerable part of the city; whoever controlled the gates controlled the city. They were mostly wooden, but often covered in bronze to protect them from fire. Because of the importance of the gates, they featured significantly in the life of the city. They had to be protected and guarded securely; they were closed and locked at night for safety. City gates were also public places: because they were the main thoroughfare they became gathering points where business was transacted. Legal judgements were made and announced there, and public disputes would be taken to the city gates. Most significantly, the elders of the city often sat at the gates dispensing justice and wisdom (see Proverbs 31:23). They were visible there, therefore everybody knew where to find them. City gates therefore came to symbolise authority and power - they are mentioned nearly 350 times in the Word of God.

The advantages of a city having narrow gates rather than wide ones are obvious: they were easier to defend, less vulnerable, and generally more secure. The narrow gate may well be more difficult to pass through than a wider one at certain times - the beginning and end of the day when many people would be coming and going, for example. Or they could get crowded because of the vast numbers gathered there for the purposes already mentioned. However, the long term benefits of a narrow gate far outweighed the easier option of a wide gate: the wide gate invited trouble and was harder to control. The wide gate might appear more attractive and make life easier; in reality it was a disaster waiting to happen. Once a city's gates were broken through by enemy attack, that city was doomed to destruction.

Now we understand the imagery Jesus uses here we are able to grasp what he means. He is contrasting the way of the kingdom of God and that of the dominion of darkness, the way of righteousness and the way of wickedness, the way of discipleship and the way of rebellion, the way of life and the way of death (he calls it 'destruction'). Contrary to some thinking, Jesus isn't advocating a narrow-minded religious way of life, devoid of any happiness, in which his disciples have to live an austere existence full of hardship and self-denial. Christianity is sometimes portrayed as dull and boring, and Christians are supposed to sit in hard pews, sing dirges, and listen to tedious sermons. Life is meant to be hard work, trying to please God and keeping oneself free from the sin that is all round us. We scrape through to heaven by the skin of our teeth. Life is one struggle after another. That is not Christianity; that is religion.

Rather, Jesus is stating the obvious in light of all that has gone before in the Masterplan. If we choose to follow him as his disciples then our lives are a complete contrast to the world - the wide gate and broad road, as he called them. To be a Christian means we choose the way - the gate - of Jesus; and in contradiction to the world the way of Jesus appears to be narrow and confined. In that sense it is. It means the end of self; it means living for him and serving him; it means living in the way he has described in his teaching; it means loving our enemies; it means embracing the kingdom of God and rejecting the ways of the world. It means depending on him for everything as the source of life; it means living by faith and and as an overcomer. It means living in the power of the Holy Spirit and being radical. It means being full of the joy of the Lord and knowing who you are. It means being a son of God. It's having all the resources of heaven right here on earth. It's being blessed and prosperous in every aspect of life. It's living the Masterplan!

The road of discipleship is 'confined' (some versions use the word 'difficult' or 'hard'); the word means to *rub together*, as things do in a tightly packed or confined space. To use a modern idiom: there is no 'wiggle room' with Jesus. If I belong to him, then I belong to him, pure and simple. Christianity is not a lifestyle in which I can do as I please. It's not about my personal self-expression or being free to be me. It is about freedom - of course it is - but I am free from sin to be a slave of Jesus Christ. That is true freedom. The wonderful thing about this 'confined' road of discipleship is that it's fantastic! I really enjoy being a Christian - my life is full of blessing. I am happy; I have a wonderful family and great friends. I belong to a marvellous church community where I am loved. I have a purpose for my life. All the promises of the Word of God are available to me. God is good to me. Why would I want to walk on a different road?

The way of the world is the way of Satan, and it's totally contrary to the way of the kingdom of God. Satan's 'gate' is wide and his 'road' is broad; this word 'broad' means *easy, flat* and is where our word 'plateau' comes from. It's also linked to the word for destruction in the New Testament, including the final judgement of the sinner to hell. This term in the New Testament means *ruination*; people ruin their lives as a consequence of rejecting the Gospel. Anyone who rejects the offer of eternal life and to be part of God's glorious family decides on the wide gate and broad road to their ultimate utter ruination - eternity spent away from the presence of God in hell. Be assured: the devil will make the road to hell as easy as he can - broad and wide - for those who want to go there. That is why Jesus warns us: don't choose that broad road. Don't go through that wide gate.

Elsewhere in the New Testament Jesus uses the same imagery with other terms to show us that he's speaking about himself as the

Gate in this passage. In John 10:7-9 he describes himself as the gate or door for the sheep: *'I am the door. If anyone enters by me he will be saved and will come in and go out and find pasture'* (John 10:9). Jesus also says of himself: *'I am the way, the truth and the life. No one comes to the Father except through me'* (John 14:6).

Jesus is the only way to God the Father; there is no other way. That is an exclusive statement from the Lord and Saviour of the world, from the King of the kingdom. However, Jesus isn't only the Way to the Father - he is the Way in everything we are and do. He is every choice we make, every value we embrace, every thought we think, every word we speak, every road we take. His way is our way. He is the Gate.

Consider/Discuss

How liberating is it to know that the narrow gate leads to a full life?

What do you enjoy about your life?

THIRTY EIGHT

BITTER FRUIT

Beware of false prophets who come to you in sheep's clothing but inwardly are ravaging wolves. You'll recognise them by their fruit. Are grapes gathered from thorn bushes or figs from thistles? In the same way, every good tree produces good fruit, but a bad tree produces bad fruit. A good tree can't produce bad fruit; neither can a bad tree produce good fruit. Every tree that doesn't produce good fruit is cut down and thrown into the fire. So you'll recognise them by their fruit. (Matthew 7:15-20)

In the second of his concluding statements Jesus warns us about those who come among God's flock pretending to be sheep, but who in fact are wolves. They are bent on destroying the lives of people, and, more importantly, the testimony of Jesus. I love the simplicity of Jesus' illustration. Bad plants and bad trees produce bad fruit; good plants and good trees produce good fruit. Many plants and trees produce fruit that to the naked eye look tasty and nutritious; in reality one bite will kill you. The Caribbean manchineel or beach apple, for example, looks like a tangerine and is quite tasty; but even to touch the fruit or the tree it grows on can be very dangerous. The manchineel looks harmless, but it's a killer. Jesus reminds us there are people like that; he calls them false prophets.

    Not surprisingly the Word of God contains many warnings about false prophets, because a prophet or somebody who exercises the gift of prophecy speaks the word of God. A false prophet is not somebody who merely gets a prophecy wrong: a believer can genuinely make a mistake and 'prophesy' when in fact they are just speaking out of their own spirit or mind. That is why all prophecy must be judged by others in the church who are competent to do so. Jesus is speaking about something far more sinister than somebody who makes a mistake in prophesying: he warns about those who prophesy falsely, those whose hearts and motives are at best mixed and at worst, evil.

A false prophet can prophesy something true. That might sound like it's a contradiction, but the Word of God tells us so. Therefore we have to be on our spiritual toes all the time. Just because something that somebody prophesies comes true, it doesn't mean the person who prophesied it is genuine. The example of Balaam in Numbers chapters 22-24 demonstrates that, as do passages like this:

If a prophet or someone who has dreams arises among you and proclaims a sign or wonder to you, and that sign or wonder he has promised you comes about, but he says, 'Let us follow other gods,' which you have not known, 'and let us worship them,' do not listen to that prophet's words or to that dreamer. For Yahweh your God is testing you to know whether you love Yahweh your God with all your heart and all your soul. (Deuteronomy 13:1-3)

We cannot stress this point strongly enough. We have to look beyond the words - the outward appearance - and know what is in a person's heart. That is why the church needs the Holy Spirit gift of distinguishing spirits (1Corinthians 12:10). We have to be able to know what kind of spirit is at work in someone - the Holy Spirit; the human spirit; even demonic spirits. Jesus returns to what he said earlier about judging others - he tells us to examine the 'fruit' of those who claim to speak for God. I am really grateful that I belong to a church community which takes great care to protect us in this regard.

Before we look at others we have to ensure that we ourselves are genuine, that there is nothing false or hypocritical about us. Am I a sheep or a wolf? At the same time we also have to be wise and astute regarding others. The New Testament writers warned the church about those who would seek to destroy the faith of God's people. The most successful attacks on the early church always came from within, from those purporting to be genuine but who were false. They were impostors. Therefore, Jesus twice admonishes us: 'you'll recognise them by their fruit.'

What is 'fruit?' Our answer immediately leads us to Galatians 5:22-26, which speaks about the fruit of the Holy Spirit. This fruit describes the personal qualities of the Spirit of Jesus and therefore of Jesus himself. They are also the personal qualities of the disciple. When judging ourselves and others we hold this fruit of the Holy Spirit up against us to see how we rate; because we are spiritual we rate high. This list is not something to be attained; it's who we are in Christ. Note something important: it's the *fruit* of the Holy Spirit, not the *fruits* of the Holy Spirit. This isn't a list of personal characteristics, some of which one might have while others are absent. I can't say I am a patient person but that I am also miserable. I can't be full of faith and not be kind. That is nonsense. When it comes to considering somebody who claims to speak for God, is the fruit of the Holy Spirit evident in them? What kind of person are they? They might well preach a great word; but does their life match up?

'Fruit' is also what comes out of our mouths in our words. Jesus spoke in Matthew 12:33-37 about good and bad fruit in terms of the way we speak, and that whatever is in our hearts will come out of our mouths: *'Out of the overflow of the heart the mouth speaks'* (Matthew 12:34). In our context this is not only about speaking faith and positive things; it's the purity of the source from which somebody speaks. If the person is a 'false prophet' then eventually something will come out of their mouth that will give them away. This might be a false teaching; it could also be the constant assertion of self, a bitterness of spirit, gossip, or the tone of their general conversation which will cause the spiritual person to become unsettled or disturbed. The heart will speak - pay attention to it and judge accordingly.

We also have to consider the fruit of somebody's ministry: what do they produce? Is their ministry in line with the Word of God? Do they cast doubt on or openly deny the integrity and authority of the Word of God? To whom are they accountable? Are they independent? How do they handle money? Who are their friends? These are some of the valid questions disciples should ask when evaluating the authenticity of those claiming to serve God.

Often the false represents itself as the truth; it will sail close to the truth and even present the truth - as we have seen. The counterfeit never announces itself as such; it presents itself as genuine. That's why disciples need to be able to discern what is true and what is false, what is genuine and what is counterfeit. The devil 'trades in counterfeit currency'. Unfortunately, too many gullible Christians buy what he's selling through so-called men and women of God who are charlatans, or are people who started off well but because they are not accountable to anybody or to the community of believers have become deceived and are spreading error. One of the pressing needs of the age for the church is for the people of God to be biblically and spiritually literate. How are you going to judge whether somebody's teaching is in line with the Word of God if you never read it? It's time for the church to check the fruit bowl.

Consider/Discuss

Please look over the questions posed towards the end of the chapter and give them careful consideration.

THIRTY NINE

DOING FATHER'S WILL HIS WAY

Not everyone who says to me, 'Lord, Lord' will enter the kingdom of heaven, but only the one who does the will of my Father in heaven. On that day many will say to me, 'Lord, Lord, didn't we prophesy in your name, drive out demons in your name, and do many miracles in your name?' Then I will announce to them, 'I never knew you! Depart from me you lawbreakers!' (Matthew 7:21-23)

The third of Jesus' four concluding statements is earth-shattering. It's also entirely in keeping with all that has gone before in the Masterplan. Jesus returns us to the beginning of the Lord's Prayer: 'Father in heaven...your will be done.' For Jesus, this essential element of discipleship is so vital he brings it back again, only this time with added force. It's no good just calling yourself a disciple, a Christian, a follower of Jesus. Merely calling Jesus your Lord or Saviour counts for nothing with him or his Father. Jesus regards only those who do the will of God the Father as genuine disciples. He emphasises doing the will of the Father as the real proof of discipleship because it's how he himself lived when he was on earth. He said,

The Son is not able to do anything on his own, but only what he sees the Father doing. For whatever the Father does, the Son also does these things in the same way. (John 5:19)

Jesus was unable to do anything besides the will of the Father. Furthermore, he did what the Father did in the same way as the Father. He didn't adapt or modify the Father's will; he didn't reinterpret it for his own ends; he didn't ignore or disregard it. He did the Father's will in the Father's way; he expects us to do the same. In Luke's account of the Masterplan, Jesus also says:

Why do you call me 'Lord, Lord,' but you don't do what I say? (Luke 6:46)

Jesus' words are direct: 'You can't call me Lord and disobey me.' Some people talk about making Jesus Lord of their life; but we don't make Jesus anything. He *is* Lord - Lord of everything and everybody. Those who call him Lord obey him in their actions. They live the way he lives, otherwise he says they're not his disciples. Words without accompanying actions mean less than nothing to Jesus and the Father. For Christians Jesus is Lord in word and deed. He says to us, 'You call me Lord? Then do what I tell you, because I tell you the will of the Father in heaven.' This is what James addresses in his letter: *Don't just listen to the word, do what it says; otherwise you're deceived* (James 1:22). Even our actions in themselves don't necessarily mean we are Jesus' disciples - we have to do the will of the Father in the way the Father says, and not do what we want in our own way. This is why Jesus is shocking in his statements in this passage. On the Day of Judgement people will put up all kinds of excuses and justifications: 'We prophesied - in your name! We drove out demons - in your name! We did miracles - in your name! Let us into the kingdom of heaven!' Jesus' reply to such people should cause us all to stop in our tracks and check our motives, plans, ambitions, visions, aims and activities. He says to them: 'I don't know you. Whatever you did wasn't in *my* name; you can't add my name on to your actions to give them the aura of authenticity.'

Then Jesus commands them to leave him, calling them lawbreakers. This is the same word used in Hebrews 1:9, which says of Jesus - *you have loved righteousness and hated lawlessness.* The Word of God says that Jesus hates lawlessness, he hates lawbreaking. He regards those who claim to represent him, who even use his name, but don't do his will, as lawbreakers - they don't live according to his ways and his will. He doesn't know such people; he says, 'You're not mine at all, you're not *my* disciples.' God is not impressed by our activities; merely putting his name to our enterprises, initiatives, ministries, churches, or claiming to act in his name are not enough. They mean nothing in this life and they have profound eternal consequences in the next. It's no good claiming that our actions justify God's approval and then being shocked when he rejects us. God approves, blesses and anoints only what he originates and commands. Hence Jesus' shattering words of judgement - 'I don't know you; I don't recognise you; I have no relationship with you; you're strangers to me; you're not my disciples.'

I am well aware of the tone of these words; be assured that I am speaking to myself as well as to anybody else who might happen to read them. This teaching of Jesus seriously brings the fear of God to me. It causes me to take stock of my life and carefully assess my commitment to the Master's plan. It makes me give sober, realistic thought to my ways. At the same time it also re-assures, excites and encourages me that I am able to do the will of the Father through the power of the Holy Spirit. It doesn't paralyse, it liberates. I have the Word of God to guide me; I have the fellowship of my brothers and sisters in Christ and my leaders to whom I am submitted. I am safe - and best of all, God is for me! He loves me and wants me to succeed. He is gracious and merciful; but he is serious in what he says about doing his will his way. There are eternal consequences to obeying or disobeying his will.

Genuine discipleship results in obedience. My dear friend Tony Ling once said, 'To obey God 99% is to disobey him 100%.' Genuine faith in Jesus as Lord results in our obedience to him (Romans 1:5). Obedience is unquestioning, unconditional and uncompromising; it is the normal Christian life. Disobedience to God is often accompanied by a stubborn refusal to believe him and to do his will (the Greek word is translated as both *unbelief* and *disobedience* in the New Testament - Hebrews 4:6). Unbelief/disobedience is not the same as doubt (Mark 9:24); here the father of the young boy in the grip of a demon struggles between faith and doubt. Jesus is on hand to help him and bring him to faith and to deliver his son. As we have seen many times along the way, God is concerned with our hearts. He takes the doubting heart and fills it with faith. The disobedient, unbelieving heart, however, is a different matter. It has set itself up against God and stubbornly refuses to believe him. This was the issue for the Israelites who left Egypt and failed to enter Canaan: *They were unable to enter because of their unbelief* (Hebrews 3:19).

How do we know if our faith is genuine? We do what our Lord and Master tells us. Unquestioning, unconditional and uncompromising obedience to his will is the way of his disciples. That is the kingdom of heaven on earth.

Consider/Discuss

Do you understand the difference between doubt and stubborn unbelief?

Are you doing what the Lord tells you in the way he has told you to do it?

FORTY

SOLID ROCK

Therefore, everyone who hears these words of mine and acts on them will be like a wise man who built his house on the rock. The rain fell, the rivers rose, and the winds blew and pounded that house. Yet it didn't collapse, because its foundation was on the rock. But everyone who hears these words of mine and doesn't act on them will be like a foolish man who built his house on the sand. The rain fell, the rivers rose, the winds blew and pounded that house, and it collapsed. And its collapse was great! (Matthew 7:24)

Jesus' fourth and final statement summarises the entire Masterplan. He uses the tools of contrast and comparison that he's employed many times in our studies. Jesus distinguishes between two kinds of people: those who are wise and those who are fools. He is not the first to draw this distinction. The book of Proverbs does the same, where the fool certainly does not come across in a good light. Here it's the same: for Jesus the wise person is *sensible, shrewd and prudent*. The foolish person is *stupid, a moral blockhead* (this what the Greek words for *wise* and *foolish* actually mean). Evidently, Jesus isn't afraid to use emotive language to make a point. The Jesus of the Gospels is not politically correct; he is highly confrontational and direct at times. That is definitely the case here.

Jesus believes his words are important; elsewhere in the Gospels he asserts that his words are 'spirit and life' (John 6:63). He expects his commands to be obeyed (John 14:15). When Jesus was on earth he took his own words seriously; he lived by them because they were the words of his Father. So in this last illustration in the Masterplan Jesus likens life to building a house: who in their right mind would build a house on a faulty or inadequate foundation? Of all the senseless things to do, why spend all your money, time and effort in building something that will inevitably fall down and that you know will eventually fall down? Why trust in something that when the pounding winds hit, will collapse in a heap? The house might look fantastic and have all the latest gadgets and gizmos. It might be able to withstand the occasional shake and tremor, the odd downpour or strong wind. But when the big storm hits disaster is guaranteed. To build one's house on a foundation of sand is the height of stupidity. So build your house on a foundation of solid rock.

Life will test and prove the authenticity of our claims to be genuine disciples of Jesus Christ. 'Pounding rain, rising rivers, howling winds' - these are all the circumstances of life that happen to us in varying degrees. They are life's happenings: good times, bad times, ordinary times, especially the 'storms of life' that come our way. They test the solidity of the 'house' we live in - what we have built, what we have made of our lives, our values, the things that are precious to us, our securities. The true solidity of our lives depends on the foundation we have built them on. You will never build something that lasts on a sandy, unstable foundation; eventually it will fall. However, if the foundation you're building on is solid rock, the house of your life will stand the test.

Jesus is the solid rock; he is our foundation. That is really important to grasp: our foundation is a real living, breathing Person - God the Son. Our foundation is a personal, vibrant, on-going, rock solid relationship with our Master in which we constantly hear his voice and do what he says out of loving obedience to him. The Holy Spirit builds a spiritual house (1Peter 2:4-5) on that foundation - it is a house of faith with accompanying action. The reality of the foundation is proved only when we place our faith in Jesus and when we put the words of Jesus into practice. That isn't a one-off experience: it's every day. We constantly hear what Jesus tells us and then we do what he tells us. That's why a strong relationship with the Word of God, the fellowship of the Holy Spirit and our fellow disciples, and a vibrant prayer life are vital. As we have explored the Masterplan we have increasingly discovered that theoretical Christianity counts for nothing with Jesus. It's just dead religion to him and he hates it. But he loves people who believe in him, who love him and are passionately committed to him and his cause, who live out in their everyday lives, by the spectacular ability of the Holy Spirit, all that he is and all that he stands for. That is why the epistle of James lays such great emphasis on having a faith that is full of action (James 1:22-25). Abraham and Rahab are the epitome of the person of faith; their faith was proved real by their actions (James 2:20-26). Disciples are doers of God's word; they are people of action.

As we conclude, we should take special note of the way that Matthew winds up the Sermon on the Mount, and the manner in which he describes the reaction of the crowds to what they have just been exposed to in the Masterplan:

...the crowds were astonished at his teaching, because he was teaching them as one who had authority and not like their scribes. (Matthew 7:28-29)

Jesus' teaching comes with an authority that cannot be gainsaid. His immediate hearers acknowledged that he spoke with the authority and backing of God the Father. He spoke with the same power and authority that brought the creation into being. That word 'astonished' means *to be thunderstruck, astounded, dumbfounded*. These people had never heard anything like this before; it certainly was nothing like the teaching that came from their own teachers, the scribes and Pharisees. These were life-changing words that challenged them at their core and invited them to live way beyond their normal expectations and natural abilities. Such is the effect of the Gospel of the kingdom on all who are faced with it and dare to respond in faith and submission to the Lordship of Jesus the Master. To be a disciple of Jesus means the end of ourselves; as a famous preacher once said, 'We live by the life of another.'

The Sermon on the Mount is as radical and relevant today as it was when Jesus first sat down and taught his Masterplan. Yes, it appears impossible to live such a life; yet it's the life that Jesus expects his disciples to live. That's why he has given us the Holy Spirit, the only Person who can live it. The demands of the Masterplan are the same as when Jesus first presented them. Its responsibilities have not changed; its privileges still stand; its adventures still await anybody who dares to take up the invitation and challenge of the Master: 'Follow Me.'

Consider/Discuss
Thank you for reading this book. May I encourage you to spend some time considering what it means for you to be a disciple of the Lord Jesus Christ. You might want to re-visit a particular chapter or verse. God bless you.